57 Great Math Stories
And The Problems They Present

by Dr. Debbie Haver,
Alice Koziol,
Elaine Haven,
and Dan Mulligan

illustrated by Adam Rodriguez

cover illustration by Warner McGee

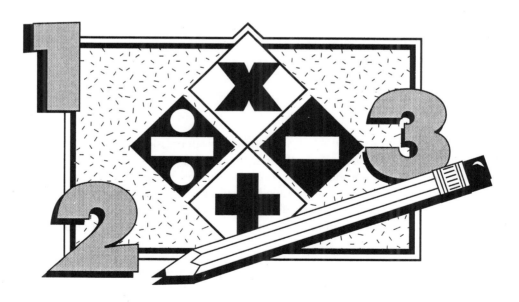

Publisher
Instructional Fair • TS Denison
Grand Rapids, Michigan 49544

ISBN: 1-56822-662-4
57 Great Math Stories And The Problems They Present
Copyright © 1998 by Instructional Fair • TS Denison
2400 Turner Avenue NW
Grand Rapids, Michigan 49544

Table of Contents

Sara's Pet 1
The Pesky Neighbor. 3
Every Girl Needs an Allowance . . . 5
Bullfrogs and Winged Bugs 7
Leo's Room 9
The Bull's-Eye. 11
School Clothes. 13
Report Card Time 15
Michael's Pentium Pro. 17
Lucky Clyde Clevermore 19
The Surprising Soccer Game 21
Eloise's Helpful Hints. 23
Go Wildcats! 25
Luciano's Pizzeria 27
A Bundle of Nerves. 29
Vinnie's New Job. 31
Surprise Birthday Party 33
Growing Gladioluses 35
The Magic Sneakers. 37
Alien Invasion 39
Vacations Are Supposed to Be Fun 41
The Teddy Bear Collection 43
Curing a Couch Potato 45
Crazy About Geometry 47
The Weirdest Emergency. 49
Jacob Asternaut's Sleep Problem. . 51
Easy Money 53
Cloud Watching. 55
Cookie on a Cattle Drive. 57

Harry's Hair Dilemma 59
Spreading the News 61
Ida Mae and the College Fund . . . 63
Sneak Previews 65
The Daytuna 500 Race 67
One Hundred Hungry Ants 69
Rocky's Roads 71
Something's Fishy 73
The Boring Trip 75
Freddie's Fertilizer 77
Cookies a Plenty 79
Nicole's Adventure 81
The Tampa Experiment 83
A Calculating Dilemma 85
Locked in the Mall. 87
The Messy Room. 89
The Combination. 91
Slammed into the Locker. 93
Travis's Dream 95
The Big Show. 97
Surfing the Deal. 99
Covering the Story. 101
Sleezy Salesman 103
Munchin' Luncheon. 105
Once on the Lips,
    Twice on the Hips. 107
Saving the Earth. 109
Tina's Mom 111
Happy Mother's Day 113
Answer Key 115

Introduction

As a result of our classroom experiences, we recognize the need to create stories relevant to the middle school student. This story problem book contains a variety of stories that will appeal to students from a myriad of backgrounds, interests, and needs. Consistent with the National Council of Teachers of Mathematics Curriculum and Evaluation Standards (NCTM 1989), our purpose is to provide opportunities for students to think creatively and to explore multiple ways of finding solutions.

> In grades 5-8, the mathematics curriculum should include varied experiences with problem solving as a method of inquiry and application so that students can:
> * use problem-solving approaches to investigate and understand mathematical content;
> * formulate problems from situations within and outside mathematics;
> * develop and apply a variety of strategies to solve problems, with emphasis on multistep and nonroutine problems;
> * verify and interpret results with respect to the original problem situation;
> * generalize solutions and strategies to new problem situations;
> * acquire confidence in using mathematics meaningfully.

The emphasis of problem solving by NCTM is deliberate. Developing problem-solving skills in students is essential in preparing them for a lifetime of real-life problem situations.

We believe all children possess mathematical power. These story problems provide the opportunity to see the mathematical strengths of all students. These strengths will be seen in the ways students invent alternative ways to solve the problems and in student contributions to group or whole-class discussion of ideas. We challenge you to spend your classroom time nurturing thinking and "pulling math out" of students instead of "pushing math in."

We are convinced that students do not learn by simply doing; they learn by thinking about and discussing what they are doing.

Achieving these goals requires you, the teacher, to create an environment envisioned by the Professional Standards for Teaching Mathematics.

> The teacher of mathematics should create a learning environment that fosters the development of each student's mathematical power by
> * providing and structuring the time necessary to explore sound mathematics and grapple with significant ideas and problems;
> * providing a context that encourages the development of mathematical skill and proficiency;

* respecting and valuing students' ideas, ways of thinking, and mathematical disposition, and by consistently expecting and encouraging students to work independently or collaboratively to make sense of mathematics;
* take intellectual risks by raising questions and formulating conjectures;
* display a sense of mathematical competence by validating and supporting ideas with mathematical argument.

This vision created by the National Council of Teachers of Mathematics requires students to use a wide variety of strategies. The following list provides the tools for students to tackle the story problems presented in this book.

Problem-Solving Strategies

Look for a pattern
Make a model
Construct a table
Make an organized list
Draw a picture
Act it out
Use objects

Correlation with the NCTM Curriculum and Evaluation Strands

The NCTM strands are listed in order of the emphasis in each story.

Sara's Pet
Patterns, Functions, and Algebra; Computation and Estimation; Measurement

The Pesky Neighbor
Computation and Estimation; Measurement

Every Girl Needs an Allowance
Computation and Estimation; Patterns, Functions, and Algebra; Probability and Statistics

Bullfrogs and Winged Bugs
Probability and Statistics; Patterns, Functions, and Algebra; Number Sense

Leo's Room
Computation and Estimation; Measurement; Number Sense

The Bull's-Eye
Number Sense; Computation and Estimation

School Clothes
Patterns, Functions, and Algebra; Computation and Estimation; Measurement

Report Card Time
Computation and Estimation; Patterns, Functions, and Algebra

Michael's Pentium Pro
Computation and Estimation; Patterns, Functions, and Algebra; Number Sense

Lucky Clyde Clevermore
Measurement; Number Sense; Computation and Estimation; Patterns, Functions, and Algebra; Geometry

The Surprising Soccer Game
Patterns, Functions, and Algebra; Number Sense; Computation and Estimation

Eloise's Helpful Hints
Patterns, Functions, and Algebra; Probability and Statistics; Computation and Estimation

Go Wildcats!
Patterns, Functions, and Algebra; Computation and Estimation; Probability and Statistics

Luciano's Pizzeria
Geometry; Measurement; Computation and Estimation; Patterns, Functions, and Algebra

A Bundle of Nerves
Computation and Estimation; Number Sense; Patterns, Functions, and Algebra

Vinnie's New Job
Measurement; Geometry; Patterns, Functions, and Algebra; Probability and Statistics

Surprise Birthday Party
Geometry; Measurement; Computation and Estimation; Patterns, Functions, and Algebra; Number Sense

Growing Gladioluses
Computation and Estimation; Measurement

The Magic Sneakers
   Computation and Estimation; Geometry; Measurement
Alien Invasion
   Computation and Estimation; Number Sense; Patterns, Functions, and Algebra
Vacations Are Supposed to Be Fun
   Measurement; Computation and Estimation; Number Sense
The Teddy Bear Collection
   Measurement; Patterns, Functions, and Algebra
Curing a Couch Potato
   Computation and Estimation; Number Sense; Measurement
Crazy About Geometry
   Measurement; Geometry; Computation and Estimation
The Weirdest Emergency
   Patterns, Functions, and Algebra; Measurement; Probability and Statistics; Computation
   and Estimation
Jacob Asternaut's Sleep Problem
   Computation and Estimation; Patterns, Functions, and Algebra
Easy Money
   Patterns, Functions, and Algebra; Computation and Estimation
Cloud Watching
   Patterns, Functions, and Algebra; Computation and Estimation
Cookie on a Cattle Drive
   Number Sense; Computation and Estimation; Measurement
Harry's Hair Dilemma
   Computation and Estimation; Patterns, Functions, and Algebra
Spreading the News
   Patterns, Functions, and Algebra
Ida Mae and the College Fund
   Patterns, Functions, and Algebra
Sneak Previews
   Computation and Estimation; Number Sense
The Daytuna 500 Race
   Measurement; Number Sense; Computation and Estimation
One Hundred Hungry Ants
   Measurement; Computation and Estimation; Number Sense
Rocky's Roads
   Number Sense; Computation and Estimation
Something's Fishy
   Measurement; Number Sense; Computation and Estimation
The Boring Trip
   Probability and Statistics; Computation and Estimation
Freddie's Fertilizer
   Measurement; Number Sense; Computation and Estimation

Cookies a Plenty

Number Sense; Computation and Estimation

Nicole's Adventure

Number Sense; Computation and Estimation; Patterns, Functions, and Algebra

The Tampa Experiment

Computation and Estimation

A Calculating Dilemma

Measurement

Locked in the Mall

Computation and Estimation; Number Sense

The Messy Room

Computation and Estimation; Number Sense

The Combination

Probability and Statistics; Number Sense; Patterns, Functions, and Algebra

Slammed into the Locker

Number Sense; Computation and Estimation

Travis's Dream

Computation and Estimation; Number Sense

The Big Show

Computation and Estimation; Number Sense

Surfing the Deal

Number Sense; Patterns, Functions, and Algebra

Covering the Story

Geometry; Measurement

Sleezy Salesman

Number Sense; Computation and Estimation

Munchin' Luncheon

Number Sense; Computation and Estimation

Once on the Lips, Twice on the Hips

Computation and Estimation; Patterns, Functions, and Algebra; Measurement

Saving the Earth

Computation and Estimation; Number Sense

Tina's Mom

Computation and Estimation; Number Sense

Happy Mother's Day

Computation and Estimation; Number Sense; Measurement; Patterns, Functions, and Algebra

The Pesky Neighbor

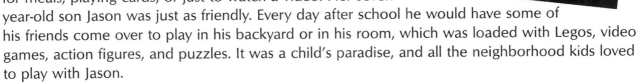

Mrs. Petrosky was a friendly person, who usually enjoyed the company of friends and neighbors. She would have friends in for meals, playing cards, or just to watch a video. Her seven-year-old son Jason was just as friendly. Every day after school he would have some of his friends come over to play in his backyard or in his room, which was loaded with Legos, video games, action figures, and puzzles. It was a child's paradise, and all the neighborhood kids loved to play with Jason.

One day a new neighbor moved in next door. Mrs. Petrosky was quick to invite the family over for a cookout. They had hot dogs, macaroni salad, and potato chips. The new neighbors, the Walters, had a four-year-old son named Patrick. "Mrs. Petrosky," said Patrick, "you make the best hot dogs in the world." Patrick had a cute impish face, with carrot red hair and blue-green eyes. Mrs. Petrosky liked him instantly even though he was a little young for her son Jason to play with. In the next few weeks Patrick kept showing up on Mrs. Petrosky's doorstep asking for water, to use the bathroom, or if she could spare a cookie. At first Mrs. Petrosky went along with Patrick's requests, but it soon became more than a little annoying—especially, when he kept asking to play in Jason's room, even though Jason was at school.

It got so bad that Mrs. Petrosky tried to avoid Patrick by not answering the door when he knocked. Patrick would then ring the doorbell in such an annoying way and for such a long time that Mrs. Petrosky would have to go out and ask him to go home. That only worked for a short time and Patrick would be back.

Eventually, Patrick started coming over and looking in the windows to see if Mrs. Petrosky was home. In the kitchen, where Mrs. Petrosky had ruffled curtains along the bottom of the window, Jason would jump up again and again to see if he could spot Mrs. Petrosky. It would have been comical if it had not been so irritating. He looked just like an excited little Chihuahua yelping to get in. This had to stop. Mrs. Petrosky decided to make bottom curtains for the whole house that would reach as high as the kitchen curtains with another four inches to keep Patrick from seeing in when he jumped.

She made the curtains and it worked for a few days. "At last, I'll be in peace," smirked Mrs. Petrosky, until she noticed Patrick running through her yard with a small wooden footstool in hand.

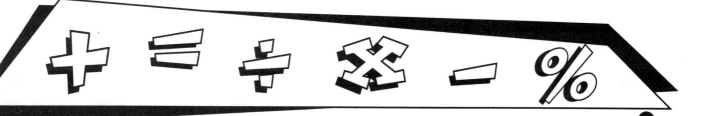

1. Mrs. Petrosky was having a cookout and she had invited all the neighbors. She had to figure out how many packages of hot dogs and buns to buy. If we figure 2 hot dogs for each person and there are 17 people, how many packages of hot dogs and buns should she buy? _____ Remember, hot dogs come in packages of 10, and buns come in packages of 8.

2. If hot dogs cost $1.89 per package and buns cost $.99 per package, what will the total cost of Mrs. Petrosky's purchases be? _____ If the buns are on sale for $.20 off the original price, and Mrs. Petrosky uses a coupon for $.25 off each package of hot dogs, how much will she spend now? _____

3. Patrick dumped one of Jason's favorite 500-piece puzzles on the floor. Mrs. Petrosky asked him nicely to pick it up, but he ran home saying, "Gotta go." If Mrs. Petrosky offered him a penny a puzzle piece to pick it up, how much money would Patrick make? _____ How many quarters would that be? _____ Dimes? _____ Nickels? _____

4. The original curtains in the kitchen were 32 inches long. Mrs. Petrosky made the new curtains 4 inches longer. How many centimeters would that be? _____

5. Mrs. Petrosky decided it would be cheaper to pay Patrick to watch their house from inside his house than to move away. She told him she had an important job for a boy detective. She would pay him a quarter for every hour he watched her house from 8:00 in the morning until 3:00 in the afternoon. If he left his post to come to her house, he would lose $.25 of his money for every time he did that. The first day he ended up making only $.75. How many times did he go to Mrs. Petrosky's house? _____ The second day he made twice as much. How much did he make? _____

Every Girl Needs an Allowance

Quintelia was a very lucky teenager.
Anything she wanted she had only to ask her parents. She did not
get absolutely everything she wanted, but almost anything within reason. Quintelia's parents
paid for her to go to the movies, bought all her clothes, and even gave her money to get a
burger and shake after school when she asked. That was the problem. Quintelia was tired of
having to ask for money all the time. Most of her friends had an allowance, and she wanted
one too. Every girl needs an allowance.

Quintelia, who had two younger sisters, was always the one who had to pave the way. When
it came to bedtimes, she pestered her parents to let her stay up till 11:00 on weekends since
she was now 12 years old. She had also been the one who asked and asked to be allowed to
stay home alone instead of going to a baby-sitter's house after school. So here was a new
battleground for Quintelia. She wanted her parents to give her a weekly allowance so she
would not have to ask for money all the time.

"Don't I keep my room clean and help with the dishes?" she asked her parents. "I work hard
at school, and I help my sisters Shawnia and Felicia with their homework. You give me the
money anyway," she pleaded. "Why can't you just give it to me on a regular basis? That might
make me more responsible. I could try to save some of the money," she added.

Finally, her parents gave in and decided to give Quintelia $20.00 a week. "You have to live
within your means," they said. "Don't come to us and say you spent your allowance and now
want money for a movie."

Quintelia spent her first allowance buying burgers and fries for her friends. After going the rest
of the week with not a penny to jingle in her pocket, she learned to be more careful. As
Quintelia said at the beginning, "Every girl needs an allowance."

1. Quintelia is 12 years old. Her sister Shawnia is ¾ of Quintelia's age. Her youngest sister Felicia is 3 years younger than Shawnia. How old are Quintelia's sisters? _____ Shawnia is also going to get an allowance, but her allowance will be 35% of Quintelia's allowance. What is Shawnia's allowance? _____

2. It cost Quintelia $4.25 to go to the afternoon movie. A medium buttered popcorn cost $2.75, and a large drink cost $2.25. How much money would she have left after going to the movies? _____ Could she go to the movies twice in one week? _____

3. Quintelia's dad has a plan for increasing her allowance as she gets older. He has agreed to increase her allowance by 8% each year. Make a table to show how much Quintelia's allowance will be every year until she is 16.

4. Mrs. Jones calls and asks Quintelia to baby-sit. The Joneses will be out from 7:30 P.M. until 2:00 A.M. Quintelia tells her that she charges $1.75 an hour until 12:00 midnight and $3.00 an hour after midnight. How much money is Quintelia expected to make? _____

5. With her extra earnings Quintelia buys her younger sisters some brightly decorated pencils. There are 2 pink, 1 red, 1 green, 1 orange, and 1 blue pencil. So they won't fight, Quintelia decides to put the pencils in a lunch bag and let her sisters choose without looking. What are the chances that Shawnia will choose a pink pencil? _____ A red pencil? _____ Once a green pencil has been taken out of the bag, what are the chances that Felicia will pick a pink pencil? _____ A blue pencil? _____

Bullfrogs and Winged Bugs

Getting the pool ready was a family affair for the Whetstones. Eleven-year-old Jerry and his younger sister Ellen could hardly wait for the weather to get warmer so they could use the pool. By mid May, Jerry and his family set aside one weekend to open the pool. Standing on two sides of the rectangular pool, they pulled off the heavy cover and laid it on the grass to dry.

Much to Jerry's dismay, the water looked gross. It was a dark putrid green; there were some dead bullfrogs floating on their backs and a scad of dead bugs. "Don't worry," said Mr. Whetstone. "Just a few weeks of using the filter and pouring in chemicals should clear up this mess." Jerry turned on the sand filter, but Dad wanted to wait a few days before adding any chemicals. The next day the pool looked even worse. There were many live bullfrogs jumping in from the diving board and the long winding slide of the pool.

Ellen, Jerry's younger sister, said that it looked disgusting. Jerry used a long-handled tool specially designed with a basket net on the end to clear out the dead bullfrogs, which were too big for the skimmers. Then he cleaned out the skimmers that were packed with bugs, both winged and wingless. He showed Ellen asking her, "Do you think there are more winged bugs or wingless bugs in the skimmer?" She did not know and did not care. "How about this question?" he asked." "How many bugs can the average skimmer take out of the pool in a 24-hour period?"

She grew tired of his morbid questions and went inside to look for her green and black two-piece bathing suit. "There are some things more important than bugs," she thought.

Eventually, after two weeks of using an array of chemicals including algaecides, baking soda, and chlorine, the pool was ready. Jerry walked around the pool looking at the crystal clear water and wanted to jump in. He could see the blue patterned floor of the pool, even at the deep end. But Dad wanted to wait until the daytime temperature reached an average high of 90 degrees for one week. Another week went by with temperatures fluctuating between 85 and 90. Jerry made a line graph and decided to keep track of the high temperatures so everyone could see it. The last week of temperatures that Jerry added to the graph were 88, 91, 94, 86, 85, 92, and 95. Would Jerry's dad let him into the pool now?

1. Make a line graph to represent the temperatures during the last week of checking the pool. What was the mean, median, and mode for the temperatures? Mean? _____ Median? _____ Mode? _____ What was the range? _____

2. In one of the skimmers, there was a total of 820 bugs. Of those bugs 75% were winged. How many wingless bugs were in the skimmer? _____

3. When Jerry first looked into the pool, there were 3 times as many bullfrogs as his age, but they were all dead. On the second day some live bullfrogs had jumped in, and there were 5 times as many bullfrogs as his age. How many live bullfrogs were now in the pool? _____

4. Jerry circled the date on the calendar that he was actually able to use the pool. He realized that the number on the calendar in the row above and diagonally to the left of the circled number was 9, and the number in the row below and diagonally to the right was 25. What date on the calendar was circled? _____ Try adding a + b and dividing that answer by 2. Try this formula using other dates on the calendar. Does it work all the time? _____

5. Jerry's dad used 2 gallons of chlorine at $3.75/quart, 1 pint of algaecide selling for $8.78 for a 2-pint container, and a ½ pound box of baking soda selling for $1.98 a pound. What was the total cost of the chemicals Mr. Whetstone used in the pool? _____ If Mrs. Whetstone found a sale the next week on a 5-gallon tub of powdered chlorine selling for $72.50, would they save money over the long haul buying it this way? _____ If so, how much would they save per gallon on the chlorine? _____
_____

6. Jerry and Ellen want to have their friends over for a pool party. Jerry has 7 friends and Ellen has 4. Mrs. Whetstone says they can only have 4 friends over at one time. So they put the 11 names in the bag and take turns drawing names. What are the chances that one of Jerry's friends will be chosen on the first draw? _____ What are the chances that one of Ellen's friends will be chosen on the first draw? _____ Try this by putting Jerry's name on 7 pieces of paper and Ellen's name on 4 pieces of paper. In your group keep track of the names that come up and the probability that either name will show up.

Leo's Room

It was a constant battle between Leo and his mother about cleaning his room. To Leo the room looked just fine and everything was where he could easily put his hands on it. To his mother it looked as though Leo threw everything up in the air and it stayed wherever it landed. Most of the time the drawers to his bureaus were empty because everything was scattered around the room. The top bunk was a handy place to throw the neatly folded underwear, shirts, and pants. The only problem was it was also a handy place for books, video games, and dirty clothes. Whenever a friend stayed over, they would just bulldoze everything down to the other end of the bed. This did not leave much room for sleeping, but they did not care.

Leo's mom had a cleaning woman who came in once a week, but when she saw Leo's room she said it would be an extra $10.00 a week to do his room. He did not want anyone touching his things anyway, so his mom just started closing the door to his room when company was coming. Occasionally, his mom would come up looking for dirty dishes, empty packages, and dirty clothes. It was not a pretty picture.

Finally, Leo's dad was tired of hearing his wife complain about Leo's room. He marched himself up to Leo's room and gave him an ultimatum. "You have two weeks to clean up this room," he said sternly. Anything that is not put away at the end of two weeks will be thrown out in the trash. Do you hear me, Son?" he asked. Leo knew his dad meant it when he used that tone of voice. Leo worked a little every evening after school, filling bag after bag with trash, putting away toys and games that he had outgrown, and actually putting his clothes away in the drawers and closet. He paid his younger sister Sharon a dollar to dust his room and to make the bed on the upper bunk.

When his dad came home from golfing with his buddies, Leo could not wait for his dad to check his room. Everything had a place, and the room even smelled good from the lemon dusting polish. Finally, Dad came in and could not believe his eyes. "This can't be your room," he said. "Where are all the dirty clothes, dusty soccer trophies, and magazines? I think you deserve a reward if you can keep it like this."

1. As a reward Leo will get an additional 25% added to his regular allowance. If the reward is $5.00, what is his regular allowance? _____ If his room is not cleaned, he will lose 25% from his regular allowance. How much will he get then? _____

2. The cleaning lady, who refused to clean Leo's room unless she made an additional $10.00, usually gets $54.00 to clean Leo's house one day a week. If it usually takes her 4.5 hours to clean a house, how much money is she making an hour? _____

3. If the cleaning of Leo's room was going to take about 12 hours and Leo knew he had 14 days to get it done, how many minutes would he have to spend each day to get it done on time? Round off the answer to the nearest minute. _____

4. Each bag of trash that was taken from Leo's room weighed 19 pounds. There were 7 bags of trash. What was the weight of all the trash in kilograms? Remember, a kilogram is a little more than 2 pounds.

   _____

5. Leo gave his sister Sharon a dollar for dusting and making his bed. If it took her 20 minutes to complete this job, how many times would she have to do this to make $50.00? _____ How many minutes would that take her? _____ About how many 8-hour days would that be? _____

6. The subscription to one of Leo's magazines is going to run out. He wants to subscribe again. The cost of the subscription is half of his regular weekly allowance plus $7.50 for 1 year. If he subscribes for 2 years, the subscription price is twice his regular weekly allowance minus $7.50. How much would Leo save in 2 years by taking a 2-year subscription? _____

The Bull's-Eye

Emery was a seventh grader who had everything going for him. He was on the school archery team, he usually got good grades, and he earned good money delivering newspapers on the weekend. Emery even had a girlfriend Ginny with whom he walked home from school every afternoon. Everything was going well, except for one thing—Sam!

Sam was Emery's younger brother who was always in his face teasing and tormenting him. Nothing escaped Sam's notice, and he told everyone who would listen about what he had seen and heard. Sam also teased Emery about holding hands with Ginny and talking on the phone with her too long.

One clear spring day Emery was out in the backyard practicing with his bow and arrows when Sam came out, letting the screen door bang loudly behind him. "Let me try to hit the bull's-eye," he demanded. "I can do it better than you."

Emery ignored his younger brother as though he were a bothersome gnat. "Leave me alone," Emery finally yelled when Sam started tapping on his shoulders from side to side. He swatted at Sam, but Sam was very agile and was able to jump away. Emery pulled a feather cropped arrow from his quiver and continued to aim his arrow into the homemade bull's-eye propped against a bale of hay. Even as agitated as he was, Emery was able to hit the bull's-eye every time he shot an arrow.

Since Sam could not get his older brother's attention one way, he decided to try another tactic. This one was certain to work. At least Sam thought so. Sam stood in a runner's stance about 15 feet beside the target. Every time he saw that Emery was ready to shoot another arrow, he would sprint across behind the target. He thought this would surely get a reaction from Emery, but no! Emery just aimed at the target with a single-minded stare with not a hint of irritation showing. As a matter of fact, it seemed to Sam that there was a slight uplifting to the corners of Emery's mouth.

This was becoming a challenge for Sam to really bother his older brother. Suddenly, he had an idea. He dashed to the target and leaned boldly over the bale of hay, so that his impish little face was staring directly at Emery. Now was his chance! Emery pulled his favorite yellow-tipped arrow from his quiver and took aim at the bull's-eye. Sam began to make faces and stick his tongue out at Emery, all the while saying, "Na, na, na, na, na, na!"

Just then a scream was heard from the direction of the screen door. "Stop!" It was Mrs. Humphrey, Emery and Sam's mother. Do you think Emery would really have shot that last arrow?

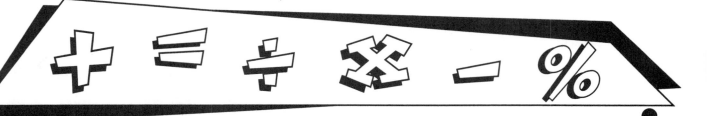

1. If the bull's-eye had points starting from the center with 50, and then 40, 30, 20, and 10, what would be the highest score that Emery could have gotten if he used 6 arrows? _____

2. Emery's arrows hit the target each time. What combinations of scores could he have hit to have a total score of 180? _____
_____

3. If Emery's total score with his 6 arrows were 140 and ⅓ of the time he hit a 50, what other area of the bull's-eye could he have hit? _____
If the total score were 160 and ⅓ of the time he hit a 40, what other area of the bull's-eye did the other 4 arrows hit? _____

4. What was Emery's total score if ⅙ of the arrows hit a 50, ⅔ of the arrows hit a 40, and ⅙ of the arrows hit a 10? _____

5. Emery's punishment was to have his allowance taken away for 3 weeks on a sliding scale. Of his $15.00 allowance, he would lose 35% the first week, 25% the second week, and 15% the third week of his punishment. How much did he lose altogether? _____ Would it have been better to lose the whole $15.00 in 1 week? _____

6. If Emery earns ⅔ more money on his paper route per week than his allowance, how much money does he earn on his paper route? _____
_____

School Clothes

It was a hot summer day in late August, and Rachel was lazing by the pool soaking up rays, so she could go back to school looking healthy and tanned. "Have you been school shopping yet?" asked Amber, Rachel's best friend. "Why don't we go together this afternoon?" she asked.

"Great!" said Rachel as she turned over and pulled up the skinny blue strap of her two-piece bathing suit. "I've only saved about $200.00 from allowances and baby-sitting this summer, so I'll have to do a lot of mixing and matching. Maybe I can weasel some more money out of my mother," Rachel mused in a hopeful way.

Back at home that afternoon, Rachel and Amber scrambled through the morning paper looking for sales at the nearby mall. A lot of stores had Back-to-School sales. "Look at this one," cried Amber. "Here's a two-for-one sale on baggy jeans. That's for me," she said, as she quickly pulled on her white sneakers and tied the pink shoelaces.

Suddenly, from the kitchen, Rachel's mother appeared with a serious look on her face. "Please get jeans that fit and tops that aren't skin tight," she said raising one eyebrow with an "I really mean it" look.

"Oh, Mom," answered Rachel. "You know it's the style right now."

Both girls hurried out the door as Rachel's mom rolled her eyes and bent over to pick up the scattered sections of the newspaper. "At least they could have picked up the newspaper," she mumbled to herself.

At the mall Rachel and Amber saw a lot of their friends hanging out, but they knew they were there to shop. So after half an hour of talking, they got down to business, walking slowly from store to store. In one store Rachel was able to get two pairs of hip-hugging jeans for the price of one. One pair was blue and the other was black. Then she picked up one red, one blue, and one yellow stretchy top. The tops were all the same price.

"Look what we've bought," yelled Rachel to her mother as she excitedly came into the quiet house. Rachel emptied the bags onto the couch to show her mother what she had bought. As her mother picked up the baggy jeans and tight stretchy tops, Rachel declared, "You'll be happy to know that I didn't spend the extra money you gave me, and I was even able to buy this long leather belt."

1. With Rachel's 2 different colors of jeans and 3 different colors of tops, how many different mix-and-match combinations of outfits would Rachel have? _____ If Rachel also uses the long belt to mix and match, how many outfits would she have now? _____

2. The 2 pairs of jeans were on sale for $50.00, buy one get the other one free. The belt cost half as much as the jeans. All 3 tops were the same price. Not counting taxes, how much did each top cost if Rachel spent exactly $120.00? _____

3. The taxes on Rachel's purchases were 7½%. How much did she pay in taxes? _____

4. If Rachel's mother had given her $30.00, how many more tops could she have bought at the same price? _____

5. Rachel bought the 2 pairs of jeans for $50.00. Amber found a pair of jeans for $27.00 with a 20% off sale. Who got the better deal on one pair of jeans? _____

6. Rachel and Amber were at the mall for 2 hours and 20 minutes. If it takes 15 minutes to walk to the mall and 15 minutes to get back, how long were they gone altogether? _____ If they left at 2:15, what time did they get back home? _____

Report Card Time

"Where's your report card, Son?" Dad asked calmly.

"Oh, the teacher forgot to hand them out," said Gabe in his most convincing voice. "I'll ask her about it tomorrow."

Gabe dashed up the stairs and into his bedroom taking a flying leap onto his bed as he heard his dad yell, "Gabe," in a loud long drawn out tone of voice.

In breakneck speed Gabe turned the volume up on his stereo. "I can't hear you, Dad," he bellowed.

Only a minute later, no it was just seconds, Dad burst into the room with his forehead all wrinkled up and his eyebrows unfurled. "Turn that horrendous music off and produce your report card immediately!" he blasted. "Your report card was due home three days ago, and all I get are excuses."

Gabe reached over, turned off the stereo, and walked across the room as if he were headed to a firing squad. From inside his old navy blue book bag, he pulled out the wrinkled envelope with his report card inside and gingerly handed it to his dad. "I was trying to wait until after the weekend in case you take away my allowance or put me on restriction," explained Gabe. "I didn't mean to lie to you."

Dad opened up the report card and stared at the grades. Gabe did well in all subjects except math. "What happened?" Dad asked. Without waiting for an answer, Dad pulled out a letter from the teacher explaining the low grade.

> Dear Mr. Francis,
>
> Gabe was doing well in math until the last three weeks. He seems to have slacked off and is not turning in his homework.
> I know if he applies himself he could raise this grade by the next marking period. Below are a list of his grades for this reporting period.
> 85, 90, 87, 95, 60, 52, 50
> Let's work together to encourage Gabe to work harder in math.
>
> Sincerely,
> Mrs. Moore

"Well, Son! What do you think would be a good punishment for the D in math?" Dad asked.

1. What is the average of all Gabe's test scores? Round it off to the nearest whole number. _____

2. If 20% of Mrs. Moore's class earned a D, how many of her 30 students earned a D? _____ What percent of her students earned a different grade? _____

3. Dad leaves the punishment up to Gabe. Either he pays his dad $.01 of allowance, with it doubling every day for the next two weeks, or he can choose to forfeit 2 weeks of his $15.00-per-week allowance. On the first day he owes Dad $.01, on the second day $.02, and on the third day $.04, and so on for 14 days. Which would you choose? _____ What is the difference between the $30.00, which is his normal 2-week allowance, and the doubling payback? _____ How many weeks would it take Gabe to pay his dad back with the doubling payback? __
_____

4. If Gabe had 2 more grades of 87 and 98 averaged in, what would his new grade be? _____

5. If Mrs. Moore let the class drop their 2 lowest grades of the original scores, what would Gabe's average be now? _____

Michael's Pentium Pro

"Dad, we need a new Pentium Pro computer," complained Michael. "I can't even play a lot of my games on this old 486." Michael loved to play computer games over the modem with his friends every day after school. His parents even had to invest in another phone line, so they could use the phone once in a while.

"A new computer would be great for you, Mom. Can't you talk Dad into getting a new computer?" whined Michael.

"I've tried," said Mom, "but you'll just have to work harder on Dad." So Michael started a one-man campaign to convince his dad that they needed a new computer very soon. Waiting was not one of Michael's strong points.

On Sunday morning, Michael looked through the Sunday paper, cutting out advertisements and information about Pentium Pro computers. He compiled all these onto a piece of yellow construction paper, making a place mat for his dad's late morning breakfast. Then on Monday he left a message on the screensaver saying, "Upgrade me to a Pentium." On Tuesday Michael reproduced a copy of his report card adding a message from the teacher that said: "Michael's progress would improve if you purchased a new Pentium Pro computer." By Wednesday Michael's dad had seen enough when he sat down to eat his breakfast and saw the words *Pentium Pro* squirted in butter on his pancakes.

"Ok, Son," he said in an aggravated tone. "Let's have a talk. I think it would be cheaper to upgrade our present computer than to buy a whole new system. Let me call around and together we'll compare the cost." On Tuesday morning the computer was in the shop awaiting a face-lift complete with a Pentium Pro chip, Windows 95, and a new mother board for a total cost of $749.00. Michael was all smiles when he finally got the computer back.

"Thanks, Dad," Michael beamed. "You made the right choice."

1. If the new computer Michael wanted was advertised in the Sunday paper for $2,809.00, and the interest on the loan was 15% per year, what would be the total cost of the computer with a 2-year loan?

_____

2. If they had bought the new computer, they would have financed it. Determine the monthly payment on the computer for a 24-month loan. Remember to add the cost of the new computer and the 15% interest per year. _____

3. Updating the computer cost $749.00. Of that $34.00 was for labor and $12.00 was for a new mouse. What was the cost of everything except the new mouse and labor? _____

4. Michael is 14 years old. His dad is twice as old plus 20 years. How old is Michael's dad? _____

5. If the cost of installing the new phone line is x squared minus 30 with x being Michael's age, how much did it cost to install the new phone line?

_____

6. Michael is quite a math whiz, but he keeps forgetting his new phone number. He created a math expression to help him remember it (555-pi 2). What is Michael's new phone number? _____

Lucky Clyde Clevermore

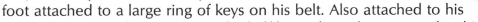

Clyde Clevermore was a very superstitious fellow. He believed there was power in blacks cats, walking under ladders, and four-leaf clovers. In fact, he always carried a lucky rabbit's foot attached to a large ring of keys on his belt. Also attached to his belt was a metal chain a foot and a half long clipped at one end to his biker's billfold. Inside that billfold was a pressed four-leaf clover that he carried everywhere.

Clyde even had a horseshoe around a horse's head tattooed to his biceps on his left arm. He loved to impress girls by jiggling the horse when he flexed his muscles. They pretended to be disgusted, but he knew they liked it.

One cold snowy day in Cleveland, Clyde won a trip to Bermuda. This was too good to be true, but Clyde had rubbed his lucky rabbit's foot again and again across the lottery ticket, so that is probably why he won. He had also been very careful in the past week around mirrors and ladders. There was only one time he got out of bed on the wrong side, but clever Clyde Clevermore jumped back in bed, fully clothed, and got out on the right side.

So on that fateful morning, Clyde waited to board the airplane to Miami and then onto Bermuda by boat. He was wearing his lucky lamb's wool vest over his one-piece sky blue jumpsuit. He made certain that one sleeve was rolled up so he could see the horseshoe and make the horse jiggle if he got scared.

Suddenly, there was a commotion in front of him. An animal carrier had fallen off a rolling cart, and a black cat scampered out onto the concourse running right across Clyde Clevermore's path. He turned around two times to the right and two times to the left and walked to his boarding gate. Waiting in line to board the plane, a woman was checking her make-up nervously in a Revlon compact. "I hate to fly," she said looking at Clyde.

"Don't worry, lady," he assured her. "I've got my lucky horseshoe." And sure enough he flexed his muscle and the horse jiggled.

She dropped her compact, and Clyde stepped on it, breaking the mirror into a zillion pieces. "Now you've done it," he said. "I'll have bad luck for seven years now." Clyde did not know if he should even board the plane, between the black cat and the mirror. Things didn't look too good. Then he looked down at his ticket—seat 13C. Clyde turned quickly, stumbling over his own feet, and ran quickly from the airport.

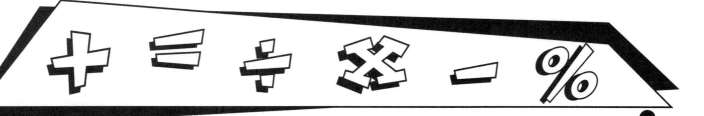

1. Clyde's tattoo had a horseshoe inside a red rectangle that was 3 inches by 4 inches. When he flexed his muscle, it would stretch to 3 inches by 5 inches. What is the difference in area of the tattoo before and after he flexes his muscle? _____

2. At the airport Clyde decided to buy a can of soda. He pulled a 1-dollar bill from his biker's billfold and put it in the machine. Out came a can of soda and 5 quarters change. This was too good to be true. So Clyde put in a 2-dollar bill, and out came 2 cans of soda and 10 quarters. How many cans of soda and quarters would probably come out if Clyde put in a 5-dollar bill? _____ 10-dollar bill? _____ 20-dollar bill? _____

3. Clyde had a strange fascination with numbers. One day he decided to mount his 4-leaf clover collection in groups of square numbers. He took a long piece of butcher paper and glue, and began this arduous task. There was 1 clover, then 4 clovers, then 9 clovers in the third set. What would be in the seventh set of 4-leaf clovers? _____ Make a table showing his collection from first to tenth.

4. In the airport gift shop, Clyde found a good luck charm to put on his large key ring. It consisted of shapes stacked one on top of the other in this order—an octagon, a nonagon, a pentagon, and a decagon. Draw a picture of his lucky charm.

5. How many sides were there altogether in all the shapes of his good luck charm? _____

Eloise's Helpful Hints

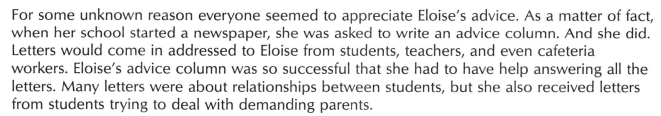

"You should wear your hair up," said Eloise smartly, as she tried to give some good advice. "And that color is all wrong for you. You should wear pastels." Eloise was a short, good-looking girl who always seemed to know what was in and what was not. Her mother owned a dress shop, and this made Eloise an instant expert on the fashion trends of the day. But Eloise's advice did not stop there. She also seemed to be an expert on relationships.

For some unknown reason everyone seemed to appreciate Eloise's advice. As a matter of fact, when her school started a newspaper, she was asked to write an advice column. And she did. Letters would come in addressed to Eloise from students, teachers, and even cafeteria workers. Eloise's advice column was so successful that she had to have help answering all the letters. Many letters were about relationships between students, but she also received letters from students trying to deal with demanding parents.

From the cafeteria workers she had letters inquiring about how to lower the noise level, reduce waste, and increase the number of lunches sold in the cafeteria. Her helpful hint for the last problem was to add a salad bar and a sandwich bar.

One of the letters was from a teacher who wanted to know how he could motivate his students to do their homework. Eloise's answer was to offer incentives, give only meaningful homework, and praise those who did the work well. Letters like these were easy, but sometimes Eloise was stumped with a letter that she was not certain how to answer. She would ask the other students who would help her, and she would even ask the advice of some of her teachers. Here is one such letter.

Dear Eloise,

Help! I'm drowning. My parents expect me to be perfect. I have to dress a certain way, get all A's, take piano lessons, compete in gymnastics, and spend my evenings with them.

I'm an only child, and I know my parents love me, so I don't want to hurt their feelings. However, I want to choose my friends, and I don't want to be the perfect person they expect. Please help me, Eloise.

Drowning at Century Middle School

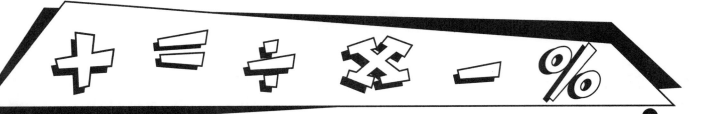

1. If the new sandwich bar at Century Middle School offered 2 kinds of bread, whole wheat and white, and 3 kinds of meat—turkey, ham, and salami, how many different combinations of sandwiches could be made? (Each sandwich can only have 1 type of meat.) _____

2. If they added 2 kinds of cheese, provolone and American, how many different sandwiches could be made? _____

3. The teacher wants to keep track of those who turn in their homework, so he makes a chart. Of his 35 students in one class, the number who turn in their homework on a typical week looks like this.

Monday	Tuesday	Wednesday	Thursday	Friday
29	32	28	30	32

   What is the mean, median, and mode of those turning in their homework? Mean? _____ Median? _____
   Mode? _____ What is the range? _____

4. Drowning at Century Middle School practices the piano for 1 hour, does homework and studying for 1½ hours, and practices gymnastics at the gym for another hour every weekday. What percent of her day is spent at these activities? _____

5. If she gives up gymnastics, what percentage of the day will her remaining activities occupy? _____

6. On one particular day, Eloise received 26 letters. If it takes her an average of 1½ minutes to read each letter, at what time should she start reading to be done at 3:30? _____

Go Wildcats!

According to *Baseball America* magazine, Great Bridge High School's baseball team was ranked fifteenth in the nation. *USA Today* ranked GBHS as twentieth in the country. It was a banner year with two of the finest pitchers the team had ever had and team members that worked well together. It seemed that everything they touched turned to gold.

John Curtice, a senior, was one of the star pitchers on the team. At 17, he was also one of the younger players, but you would never know it by looking at him. He was 6 feet 2 inches of muscle and brawn, and he had a left-handed pitching arm that was phenomenal. To some it seemed his pitching arm had the force of a jack hammer.

Whenever he was on the pitcher's mound getting ready to pitch, you could see a line of scouts raising their radar guns in unison, like the legs of a dancer in a chorus line. They were clocking the speed of John's ball as it came at the batter. It was faster than a falling meteor, it was faster than a speeding train, it seemed to be faster than a hummingbird's wings.

At one particular game on a cold windy day, it seemed their luck had changed. Everything went wrong that could have gone wrong. It was an away game, and as the Great Bridge Wildcats piled into the bus, they heard a hissing sound as one of the rear tires slowly, but surely, deflated. After changing buses and transferring all the equipment, they arrived just in time for the game. One of the best Wildcat batters fell getting off the bus and landed squarely on his shoulder, popping it out of place. What else could happen now!

The score was tied 6 to 6 in the bottom of the sixth inning. "John," bellowed the coach, "Let's get 'em out." The pressure was on, but John could handle it. With pitches averaging 91 miles per hour, John easily struck out the first two batters. "One more to go," he thought. And then it happened. John threw the ball and with a crack of the bat, the ball came barreling back at John, hit the bottom of his glove, and popped up into the air. John looked up, but he could not see a thing with the sun shining in his eyes. He stood there hopefully with his glove opened, but to his shock the ball missed his glove and plopped into his open bare left hand. The team went on to win the game 7 to 6. Go Wildcats!

1. After the win, the coach decided to treat them to a meal at Chesapeake Pizza to celebrate. The coach asked, "How many pieces of pizza will we get with 10 cuts?" _____ Make a table and see if you can find a pattern.

2. Using the radar gun, one scout found the speed of John's pitches. In his little notebook he wrote 90, 93, 91, 94, 98, 93, 95. What was the average speed of John's pitches during this game? _____

3. The coach noticed that the Wildcats had only lost ⅐ of the games they had played so far this season. Change this number into a decimal. Look for a repeating pattern and extend the digits out to 12 places after the decimal place._____

4. Determine John's batting average so far this season. In 27 times at bat John had 11 hits. To get the answer, take the number of hits and divide it by the number of times at bat. Use the first 3 numbers after the decimal point._____

5. During practices ¹⁄₁₁ of the players showed up late. What is the repeating decimal for this fraction?_____

6. John's number on his bright green jersey is 2x - 2. The variable x is more than 10, but less than 14. What are the possible numbers on John's jersey? _____ John's actual number is the median number. What is it? _____

Luciano's Pizzeria

Tony Luciano's Uncle Franko owned a pizzeria in the heart of New York City in an area called "Little Italy." It was a little place called Luciano's tucked quietly between the E-Z Care Laundromat and Pavarotti's Italian

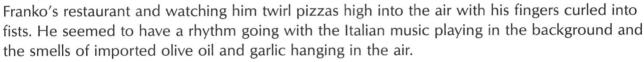

Bakery. Ever since he was a little kid, Tony loved going down to Uncle Franko's restaurant and watching him twirl pizzas high into the air with his fingers curled into fists. He seemed to have a rhythm going with the Italian music playing in the background and the smells of imported olive oil and garlic hanging in the air.

"What are you doing, Uncle Franko?" asked Tony as he walked into the pizza parlor. "You look tired and hot sitting there in the corner."

"Come here, Antonio," Uncle Franko said in his raspy voice. "We need to have a talk. I'm getting old and I need to have some help. Would you like to work with me afternoons after school and weekends? I'd teach you everything you need to know."

"Would I!" said Tony excitedly. "I'd love to," he added. And so his education began. One of the hardest things was learning to twirl pizzas and to get them the right size. The first few pizzas ended up on the floor. One pizza even ended up hitting the fan blades when he threw it up too high. That was a sight with sheets of dough hanging from the blades, and then being thrown out around the room. Some dough barely missed hitting a customer who was standing near the cash register.

But eventually, Tony improved and he even got to the point where he would show off when there were customers in the store. He would throw the pizza up with a twirl of one hand and catch it with the other hand, looking as though he had been doing it all his life.

The local Boys' Club called in an order. Tony picked up a stubby yellow pencil and began to take the order. "We'll have two large pepperoni pizzas, three large pizzas with sausage and peppers, two large cheese pizzas, and a large Luciano Special. Someone will be in to pick them up in about an hour," the caller said.

"No problem," Tony answered as he wiped his brow. Uncle Franko returned just then in time to help with the order.

1. Tony had trouble making all the large pizzas the same size. The largest pizza that could fit in the box would have a diameter of 16 inches. What would the circumference be? _____

2. If a medium pizza had a circumference of 43.98 inches, what would the radius of the pizza be?_____

3. The Boys' Club ordered 2 large pepperoni pizzas, 3 large pizzas with sausage and peppers, 2 large cheese pizzas, and a large Luciano Special. A large cheese pizza at Luciano's cost $7.99 and each extra topping cost $.75 more. The Luciano Special cost twice the price of a cheese pizza. How much is the tab for the Boys' Club? _____

4. Uncle Franko gives the Boys' Club a discount of 12% on all purchases. How much do they actually owe before taxes? _____ Food tax here is 8%. Total the entire bill, adding the 8% food tax at the end. What is it?

_____

5. Tony has to deliver pizzas in the neighborhood. Uncle Franko has a sense of humor and he also wants to help Tony with his math, so he tells him the street name, but not the house number of customers. Instead he gives him clues. Try to figure out the addresses of these orders by solving for x.

$2x + 6 = 12$ 5th Street
$4(x + 1) = 20$ Napoli Avenue
$x^2 + 3 = 52$ San Paolo Street
$\dfrac{x + 3}{2} + 4 = 16$ Italiano Avenue

A Bundle of Nerves

Buffy Boitano was a middle school math teacher who was getting ready to attend her first math conference in Minnesota. She was all excited about going, but she was frightened of flying. Her friend Diane was going with her, so that would be some comfort.

That morning she was a wreck. Buffy had not slept at all that night, so she drank plenty of black coffee until Diane showed up to take her to the airport. The traffic was backed up at the exit ramp. "It'll be fine," Diane said as Buffy sat wringing her hands with her eyes darting from side to side. "Just relax."

"I'm relaxed," Buffy retorted nervously. "Don't talk to me." They checked in, just in time. As they boarded the plane, Buffy noticed two workers playing around with the onboard computer system. "What's happening?" Buffy asked Diane.

"Oh, it's probably nothing," said Diane.

Just then the captain came on the intercom and announced, "We're having computer problems and the plane will be delayed while it is being worked on."

Buffy's stomach started to tighten into a knot. Her nails had paved grooves into the palms of her clenched fists, and the left side of her face had developed a strange tic. She was as white as a sheet. "I don't know if this trip was a good idea," she whispered nervously to Diane.

The plane finally took off with Buffy white knuckled, clenching the armrests of her seat. She looked neither to the right, nor to the left, but stared straight ahead. Her eyes were opened wide, and it seemed to Diane that she rarely blinked. "Are you all right?" Diane asked worriedly, as the plane pitched and rocked with turbulence.

After a bumpy one-hour flight, the plane landed in Minneapolis. Still Buffy was staring straight ahead in a catatonic state. After everyone else had deplaned, Diane had to peel back Buffy's fingers one by one. Diane and the flight attendant helped Buffy off the plane. "Will you be needing a wheelchair?" the flight attendant asked.

"Not for me," said Buffy walking off as though nothing had happened. "Where is the baggage check?"

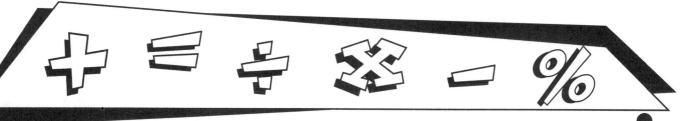

1. Diane noticed that of the 10 cars waiting at the exit ramp on the highway, ⅗ of them were white. How many white cars were there?

   _____

2. As Buffy was sitting nervously on the plane, her eyes were darting from side to side. She tried to focus on math to take her mind off her fear of flying. She noticed that ½ of the passengers were men. Of the men ⅔ of them were bald. What is ⅔ of ½? _____ If there were 90 people on the plane, how many of the male passengers were bald? _____

3. Someone had changed the keys on the keypad of the onboard computer. The repairman knew the vowels were correct, but all the consonants had been switched. This is the message they typed to decode and replace the keys. Can you figure out the message?

   ZASMEZASIXP IP JUT!

   One other clue is that the first word starts with an M. _____

   _____

4. The first estimate was that the flight's takeoff would be 15 minutes late. Actually, they were 20% later than this. How late was the flight?

   _____

5. At the baggage claim, Buffy lifted her luggage off the revolving conveyor belt. Of the 3 pieces of luggage, the larger suitcase was 15 lbs. heavier than the medium-sized luggage. The smallest piece of luggage was 10 lbs. lighter than the medium size luggage. If the total weight of her luggage was 80 lbs., how much did each piece weigh?_____

6. Diane noticed that Buffy's finger was jerking in a pattern when she was on the plane. The pattern looked like this: 1, 4, 9, 16. How many times will Buffy's finger jerk next if she continues in this pattern? _____

Vinnie's New Job

The sign said, "Wanted—Young Clean-cut Cook,—will train as an omelet maker." Vinnie Tarantino read the sign and thought, "I can do that." He had worked at his Uncle Tito's neighborhood grill in the Bronx. After applying, he was hired on the spot.

There were just a few problems with the job. He had to wear a white double breasted jacket over his baggy jeans and sweatshirt and a tall cylindrical chef's hat which would mess up his hair. They also asked him to wear less of his gold jewelry, including the gold ring in his nose. He really needed the job, so he complied.

On the third day of his training, Vinnie was left alone at the omelet station. There were four burners that he was expected to work, all at the same time. Behind the burners were plastic bins of mushrooms, onions, ham, green peppers, tomatoes, and cheese. Too many choices, if you asked Vinnie. He was trying to juggle four omelets, all at the same time, when things started to go wrong. He noticed one of his long curly hairs had gotten into one of the omelets. "I guess I'll trash that one," thought Vinnie. "Oops! There goes the spatula."

As Vinnie bent over to pick it up, he knocked over the pitcher of beaten eggs, all over his double breasted jacket. He tried to clean it up, but in the meantime one omelet was burning, the omelet line was getting longer, and he was getting some dirty looks from the customers.

Then to top everything off, a rather large gray-haired lady muscled her way to the head of the line with her omelet in hand. "Young man," she said in a snippy tone of voice, "I asked for an omelet with everything except tomatoes. You put tomatoes in this omelet." Vinnie grabbed the plate, picked the tomatoes out with his fingers, and handed the plate back to her. She gasped and said loudly, "I want to see the manager."

"Hey, lady, you can have my job. I quit!" Vinnie snapped as he quickly tore off the coat, slapping it onto the floor, threw down his chef's hat, stomping it as he walked off, and said, "This guy has cracked one too many eggs!"

1. The top of Vinnie's hat had a radius of 3. What was the circumference of the top of his chef's hat? _____

2. If each omelet has 2 fillings (excluding cheese), how many different combinations of omelets are possible? _____

3. Vinnie was making $7.20 per hour as an omelet maker. How much was that per minute? _____ If Vinnie worked 5 days a week for 8 hours per day, and 28% of his earnings were taken out for taxes and insurance, what would Vinnie's take home pay be per week? _____

4. The number of eggs used for omelets varies daily. In one week Vinnie cracked the following number of eggs.

Monday	Tuesday	Wednesday	Thursday	Friday
183	212	227	243	198

   What was the average number of eggs that Vinnie cracked per day? _____ How many dozens of eggs should the restaurant buy for omelets Monday through Friday? _____

5. The largest number of omelets is sold on Sunday morning. If it takes 6 minutes to make an omelet and 216 omelets are made, how long will that take in total minutes? _____ Remember there are 4 omelet pans going at one time. How many hours will that be? _____ At what time would he have to start to be done by 1:00?

   _____

Surprise Birthday Party

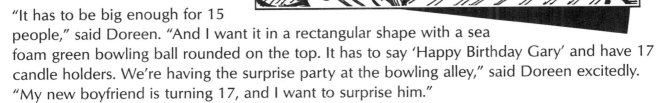

"What size cake do you want?" asked the woman behind the counter.

"It has to be big enough for 15 people," said Doreen. "And I want it in a rectangular shape with a sea foam green bowling ball rounded on the top. It has to say 'Happy Birthday Gary' and have 17 candle holders. We're having the surprise party at the bowling alley," said Doreen excitedly. "My new boyfriend is turning 17, and I want to surprise him."

"No problem," assured the woman. "I can use a bowl to make the bowling ball shape. It'll be ready. Look around. We have a lot of party supplies." Doreen found noisemakers, corny hats, and napkins. She was determined to surprise Gary this time with all of their best friends. Everyone was sworn to secrecy. The party would be two weeks before Gary's actual birthday, so that should help to make it a surprise.

Then Doreen went shopping for presents. "I'm determined to make his birthday special," she thought. So she shopped and shopped until she found the perfect gift for Gary—a gift certificate to Sports America. "How can I wrap this so it looks impressive?" she wondered. Then she had an idea. Gary was a great practical joker, so he would appreciate this. She put Gary's present in the middle of a paper towel tube and stuffed the space with tissue paper. Then she found a long rectangular box and placed the cylinder inside. She then placed the rectangular box into a large square box, which she then sealed and wrapped with ribbon and a large blue box.

Doreen decorated the party room at Jax Bowling Alley with streamers, balloons, and signs. Everything was ready as Gary's friends started to arrive. "I didn't know it was Gary's birthday," said Shawna. "It seems like we just had a party for him last summer."

Just then Gary walked in laughing with his best friend Max. Everyone yelled, "Happy Birthday!"

"Whose birthday is it?" asked Gary.

"Didn't you tell me it was your birthday on the first day of April?" asked Doreen in a worried voice. "Oh that," said Gary. "April Fools."

"Well, here's your April Fool's gift," she said as she picked up the large wrapped present and threw it at him, narrowly missing his head.

1. The cake Doreen ordered was 6 inches by 12 inches. The bowling ball had a diameter of 4 inches. What was the surface area left for writing "Happy Birthday Gary"? _____

2. Doreen bought a gift certificate to Sports America for $25.00. She spent 21% less for the birthday cake than the present. How much did the cake cost? _____

3. There was a strange formula for figuring out the price for the writing on the cake. Vowels cost 2 cents for the first vowel, doubling the cost for every vowel after that. Consider the letter y as a vowel. Consonants cost 3 cents a piece. How much did the writing cost? _____

4. To wrap the large box, which was a cube, Doreen had to know the surface area. If the length of one edge of the large box was 30 inches, how much paper does Doreen need to cover all the surfaces?

   _____

5. Doreen found a bag of giant colorful balloons with a price tag of $4.50 for 20 balloons. She found another bag for $6.00 for 24 balloons. Which is the better buy? _____

6. There will be 15 people at the party. Each small table holds 4 people. How many tables will they need? _____ If they put the tables together into 1 long table, how many small tables will they need? _____ Draw a picture to show your answer.

Growing Gladioluses

Dave and Herm were teenagers who lived on their parents' farm in Edwardsburg, Michigan. "How can we earn some extra money?" they asked their dad. "We tried raising chickens last year, but they all froze to death," lamented Dave. "Then there were the rabbits we raised, but they multiplied so fast, and we couldn't find anyone who wanted to buy them."

"Yeah," said Herm. "I remember Mom making rabbit stew, fried rabbit, and rabbit au gratin till I felt like I would grow a cottontail. We lost money on that deal after paying for sacks of rabbit pellets. The cleanup kept us hopping, too."

"I want to try something that doesn't bite or eat," said Dave to his older brother. "Why don't you try growing gladioluses?" suggested his mom Bonnie. "You could use the old wooden stand Grandpa built years ago to sell the gladioluses. It's out behind the pole barn right now," she added.

So Dave and Herm started their new venture by ordering gladiolus bulbs from Baumberger's Feed and Seed down in the village. They were not certain if growing and selling flowers was a manly thing to do, but they had run out of good ideas.

When it was time to plant the bulbs, Herm rode the tractor to plow the rows. Dave walked behind the tractor carrying a heavy feed sack of gladiolus bulbs, bending over to drop one bulb at a time every so often. It was hard work for Dave, and he was at it long after dark, while Herm parked the tractor beside the root cellar and went off to shoot some hoops with his friends.

"Why don't you help me with the watering, weeding, and hoeing?" Dave asked Herm. "It wouldn't take so long if you would help."

"I'm too busy," said Herm. The bulbs grew into handsome green stems, and finally the day came when the flowers started to bloom. Dave cut the flowers, placing them into old milk cans at the stand in front of his house.

"Let me help you put up the sign, Son," said his dad. "Where's Herm?" Isn't he supposed to be helping you?"

"Sure thing," said Dave, "but he says that's what younger brothers are for. The only thing he did was to plow the gladiolus field. That night at the farm house Herm came up to Dave with his hand held out for his share. "Here's $2.00," said Dave.

"Is that all we earned?" asked Herm disappointedly.

"No," said Dave. "That's what you earned."

1. It took Herm 2¼ hours to plow the gladiolus field. How long did it take to plow ⅚ of the field? _____

2. You can buy gladioluses in bulk bulbs for $.18 each for any amount from 1 to 1,000, or you can buy the Gardener's Pack—25 bulbs per pack for $5.99. If Herm and Dave wanted to plant 500 bulbs, which would be the better buy?_____

3. A 3-lb. box of bulb booster fertilizer cost $3.36. How much is that per ounce? _____

4. In one area of the field, Dave planted 5 long rows. He took these notes so he would remember where the different colored gladioluses were planted. The red gladioluses were next to the blue gladioluses. The yellow gladioluses were in the last row, and the purple gladioluses were in the first row next to the orange gladioluses. The red gladioluses were not in the middle row. In what order were the colors?

   _____

5. Dave and Herm sold their fresh gladioluses for $1.50 per dozen. At the end of the day they sold the leftovers for ⅓ off the regular price. What was the new price at the end of the day? _____

6. The entire gladiolus business venture took ⅙ of the year. How many months was that? _____

The Magic Sneakers

Edward Gluck, a young man, had just witnessed an amazing display of magic from a wandering magician on the streets of New York City. "How did you pull that silver dollar out of your ear?" he asked in a very gullible way.

"Oh, it's easy," said the magician, noticing Edward's brand new Nike sneakers. "You see these old worn out sneakers I'm wearing? Well, they're magic sneakers and they make you lucky," he said slyly. "But I've had all the luck I can stand for one day. You're about my size. I'd be willing to trade them for your sneakers."

"Wow!" said Edward sincerely. "Let's do that." On the way home Edward noticed a navy blue lady's purse in a wire trash bin in front of his house. The only thing left in it was a checkbook, pictures, and credit cards. He turned it right in to the police.

"These sneakers really are magic," he said to the magician. "I got a $10 reward for turning in a stolen purse."

"If you think that's great," said the street magician, "you should be wearing my old magic coat."

Edward quickly took off his New York Giants jacket as he said, "I'll trade." Edward put on the ratty torn nylon jacket from the magician. "I feel lucky," said Edward as he walked away whistling.

"Look at this, Mom," he said, as he unwrapped a candy bar later that afternoon. "It says I've won $100. Just wait till I tell the street magician."

"You what!" said the magician shocked. He knew his things were not magic and did not bring luck. This was just a coincidence. "Do you want to trade your baseball cap for my old green knitted hat?" Edward looked at the ragged hat that had seen better days, but he said, "Yeah! OK."

That afternoon Edward's mom was aghast when she answered the door. It was a registered letter. As she opened the envelope and read the letter, she dropped down to the couch in shock. It read, "You are the proud winner of $10,000."

The next time Edward saw the magician, he told him of his good luck. "Please return my things," the magician pleaded with Edward. "It wasn't fair to give you my old ragged sneakers, jacket, and hat for your new things."

1. The sneakers had been on sale for 20% off the original price of $79.95. If Edward's mom made him pay ¼ of the final price with his allowance, how much did Edward pay on the final price of the shoes? _____

2. The police asked Edward, "What was the time when you found the purse in the trash can?"

   He said, "It was after lunch and the hands of the clock made a right angle like this 'L.'" What time could it have been?

   _____

3. The magician's ratty torn jacket had a hole in the shape of a rectangle. It was 2¼ cm by 1⅓ cm. What was the area of the hole? _____

4. Since the magician had given Edward the magic sneakers, jacket, and hat, he asked Edward to give him a percentage of his winnings. The street magician asked for 45 percent of the total amount Edward had won. How much was he asking for? _____

5. Edward, being such a good person, decided to return all of the magician's clothes and give him ⅓ of the winnings. How much money did Edward give the magician? _____

Alien Invasion

"Learn all you can about these earthlings, and we'll be back to pick you up in about five days," said Moro to Zorax. "We have to know if they would be compatible with our people," said Moro. "But whatever you do, don't eat their food. It could be poisonous to us."

Zorax leaped out of the spacecraft just seconds before it took off at supersonic speed. When he saw his first earthling, Zorax was surprised. "Man, oh man! Where did you come from?" cried Steve in his backyard.

"Do you see that star?" Zorax asked pointing up. "That's close to where I come from. I'm here to learn about you earthlings."

"We've got to find a way to hide you while you're here," said Steve. "Come on up to my room. You're a little smaller than me, but it's the style to wear baggy clothes." Steve also put dark sunglasses on Zorax to hide his weird catlike eyes. "Now you'll fit right in as one of my friends," said Steve. "Just try not to talk too much."

Steve led Zorax into the living room where his parents and little sister were sitting in the dark, watching television. "Mom, Dad, this is my friend Zorax."

"Hi, Zorax," said Dad glancing over at the strange-looking kid. "Want some frozen pizza?"

"Sure, Dad," said Steve answering for Zorax. Zorax was tempted by the smell of the pizza, and he ate two slices in spite of Moro's warning. "It looks harmless," he thought.

By the time Moro returned to pick up Zorax, Zorax was having a great time eating burgers, fries, shakes, and chocolate candy. That was his favorite.

"What happened to you?" asked Moro. "You look like you've gained 20 pounds in these five days."

"The food was good," bragged Zorax. "And I've learned a lot. Earthlings eat all the time, wear clothes that don't fit, and spend time sitting in front of a box that they can't communicate with. The worst part is the loud music that they use to drown out the sound of someone talking. I don't think our people would like it here," said Zorax as he hid a pack full of chocolate candy bars behind his back.

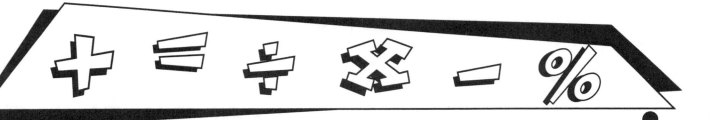

1. Steve made his favorite fruit juice for Zorax. He mixed ¾ ounce of kiwi juice and ⅙ ounce of papaya juice. What was the total weight of the juice? _____

2. Steve had $2.00. He spent ⅘ of that money when he went out for a burger and fries. How much did he spend? _____

3. Zorax was on earth for 5 days. What fraction of a month is that considering a month has about 30 days? Reduce to lowest terms.

   _____

4. Moro's spacecraft could travel at 954 miles per hour. How many days would it take to go 137,376 miles? _____

5. In Zorax's pack of candy bars, he had 7 bags of M & Ms at $.59 each, 3 Hershey bars at $.79 each, and 15 packages of Sweet Tarts at $.39 each. How much did all the packages of candy cost? _____

6. The number of people on Zorax's planet is 7 to the 8th power. How many people were on Zorax's planet? _____

Vacations Are Supposed to Be Fun

Ethel Pascarelli, a retired elementary teacher from Southern California, had always wanted to travel. "Now's my chance," she told Betty, the travel agent. "I want to pick up my suitcase, without a care in the world, and see the sights around the world."

"How about going to England first?" questioned Betty. "You could see Big Ben, the Tower of London, and Buckingham Palace."

"Sounds good to me," said Ethel.

Upon stepping off the plane in England, Ethel was greeted with a drizzly rain that turned into a steady stream and then a pelting downpour. She had not brought an umbrella, nor had she brought a raincoat, so she bought both of these things in Harrod's, a famous department store. She also purchased a pair of galoshes for the deep puddles she had to traverse.

"Betty," said Ethel over the phone, "the trip was a disaster. It rained all the time."

"Don't give up," said Betty. "How about Newfoundland? It's beautiful there in the spring."

"Sounds great to me," said Ethel. So Ethel went off to Newfoundland carrying her tweed suitcase, her galoshes, her umbrella, and her brown English raincoat, just in case.

The weather report was not good, but Ethel decided to make the best of it. It started to snow on the first day, and by the third day the snow was four and a half feet high. The only way to get around was to wear snowshoes, so Ethel purchased those and a warm woolen coat, gloves, hat, and an extra suitcase to hold all her purchases.

"Betty, Betty, Betty," said Ethel when she returned, "the weather was atrocious. It snowed so hard that by the fifth day the snow reached up to the windowsill of my hotel room, and I was on the second floor. I think I need a warmer climate."

"I've got just the place for you," said Betty. "How would you like to go to Hawaii? You wouldn't need the snowshoes or the umbrella. Chances are there will be sunshine day after day."

"Sounds good to me," said Ethel. So she flew to Hawaii with her old tweed suitcase.

"Why is the sky so black?" Ethel asked a waiter as she lay on the beach under a huge beach umbrella.

"M'am, that's Kilahua spewing some ash. Lava is flowing slowly down the mountainside, but I don't think it will come this far. At least not for awhile."

Ethel found the closest phone. "Betty, get me on the next flight home. I've had all the traveling I can stand in this lifetime."

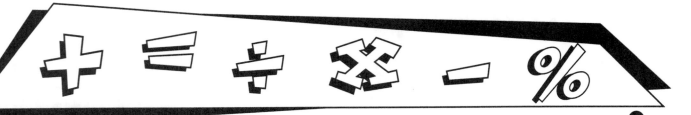

1. Ethel decided to call her sister who lived in Brooklyn, New York, while on her trip to England to complain about the weather. When it is 9:00 P.M. in New York, it is 2:00 A.M. in England. Ethel called at 7 P.M. from England. What time was it in New York? _____

2. The airline ticket to Newfoundland was ⅜ less than the ticket to England. The round-trip ticket to England cost $800. What was the cost of the ticket to Newfoundland? _____

3. In England Ethel bought a raincoat for $28.00 more than the cost of the pair of galoshes. The umbrella cost $4.00 less than the galoshes. How much did the galoshes cost? _____ The total price was $48.00.

4. In Newfoundland Ethel heard a weather report that said the normal temperature for that time of year was about 68 degrees. Instead, the temperature while Ethel was there was 29 degrees. What was the difference between the normal and actual temperatures? _____

5. By the fourth day in Newfoundland, it had snowed 5⅚ feet. By the time she left, it had snowed 10⅔ feet. How much did it snow from the fourth day to the last day? _____

The Teddy Bear Collection

Carly had a large teddy bear collection that was started on her first birthday when her Uncle Zeke gave her a stuffed Kodiak bear from his regular trips to Alaska. It was a well-loved bear, but now Carly had bears of every size, shape, and color on shelves over her bed and all around her room.

"What can I get my favorite niece for her tenth birthday?" asked Uncle Zeke.

"I want a real bear," answered Carly naively.

"I can't do that, but I can do the next best thing. I'll pick you up tomorrow after school, and I'll take you to the Teddy Bear Factory Store."

Carly entered the store with her mouth wide open. Besides the bears that were displayed around the store, there were bins of unstuffed bears in all sizes, along with bear costumes hanging on racks in the middle of the store. Carly walked around for quite a while looking in all the bins.

"Have you chosen a bear to stuff?" asked Uncle Zeke.

"I love this honey colored bear with the soft curly fur," said Carly.

"Take it over to the stuffing machine," said Uncle Zeke.

Carly held her bear up to the pipe that shot pieces of Styrofoam into the bear like stuffing a sausage. "I can feel him coming to life," said Carly excitedly. After watching her bear being sewn up, Carly went to the racks of clothes. "He'll look good in this blue and white striped train engineer's outfit with the red scarf around his neck," said Carly. "Thank you, Uncle Zeke. He really is the next best thing to a real bear."

That night Carly thought about a name for her bear. "Kodiak, that's what I'll name him," she thought. She set him on her night table and turned off the light. "Goodnight, Kodiak," she said.

"Goodnight, Carly," she heard. Carly's eyes popped open.

"Did I hear what I think I heard?" thought Carly. "Did you say something?" asked Carly looking straight at Kodiak.

"Sure, I said goodnight. Didn't you hear me?" said Kodiak.

"Stuffed bears aren't supposed to talk," said Carly. "Well, you brought me to life in the Teddy Bear Factory Store, so if you don't want a talking bear I guess you're stuck with me."

"Oh, no!" said Carly. "You're even better than a real bear."

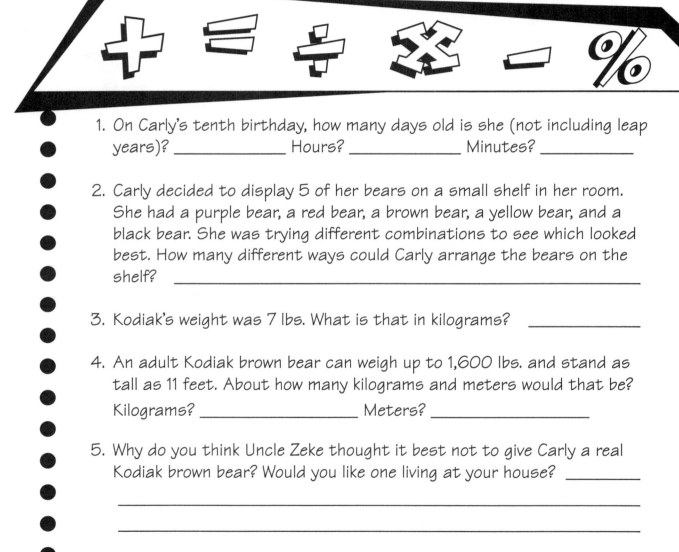

1. On Carly's tenth birthday, how many days old is she (not including leap years)? _____ Hours? _____ Minutes? _____

2. Carly decided to display 5 of her bears on a small shelf in her room. She had a purple bear, a red bear, a brown bear, a yellow bear, and a black bear. She was trying different combinations to see which looked best. How many different ways could Carly arrange the bears on the shelf? _____

3. Kodiak's weight was 7 lbs. What is that in kilograms? _____

4. An adult Kodiak brown bear can weigh up to 1,600 lbs. and stand as tall as 11 feet. About how many kilograms and meters would that be? Kilograms? _____ Meters? _____

5. Why do you think Uncle Zeke thought it best not to give Carly a real Kodiak brown bear? Would you like one living at your house? _____

_____

_____

Curing a Couch Potato

"Bring me some chips and a Coke," yelled Bill to his wife Martha. "And make it snappy," he added. "The basketball game is about to start." Martha brought the Coke and chips to Bill, and set them down on the coffee table. "You forgot the dip," Bill said irritatingly, not taking his eyes off the game for a minute. So off she went to get the dip.

"Can we go to the mall?" asked Martha. Bill didn't answer. "Bill," she called, but still he didn't answer.

Finally, she stood in front of the TV to get his attention, but all he said in a loud voice was, "Get out of the way."

Martha went off to the mall, looking in some of the most expensive clothing stores. She bought a fancy blue dress with sequins, a long suede jacket, and a pair of shoes to match the dress. "Maybe he'll notice me now," she thought.

At home she modeled her new clothes, prancing around back and forth in front of the TV. "How do I look, Bill?" she asked.

"Fine," said Bill looking from side to side to see around her.

"I spent about $800," she said.

"Fine," he said absentmindedly.

"The car was wrecked and I'm leaving for the moon," she said just to check his listening.

"That's good," he said. "Make me a tuna sandwich on rye, will ya,' Martha?"

Martha was at the end of her rope. "I need to do something more drastic," she thought. The next day when Bill came home and lay down on the overstuffed couch, he noticed that the remote control would not work. "Martha," he yelled. "Come and turn on the TV for me."

She did, but the TV was not working. "I'll call someone tomorrow," she said. "In the meantime, let's go out to the mall for dinner and to see a movie."

The next night the TV still wasn't working, so Martha and Bill went bowling. "I'm really enjoying this," said Bill. "Maybe the TV should have broken years ago. I think I was in a rut."

"That's for sure," said Martha, as she stuffed the missing TV parts deeper into her purse.

1. Bill would drink a 12 pack of cans of soda at a sitting while watching TV. How much Coke did Bill drink if each can holds 12 oz. or 355 ml?

   _____

2. Martha pays $3.99 for a 12 pack of Coke. A 2-liter bottle of Coke sells for $1.09. There are 1,000 ml in a liter. With the amount of soda that Bill drinks, would it be cheaper for Martha to buy the soda by the 12 pack or 2-liter bottles? _____ How much of a difference is there? _____

3. Martha decides to make Bill a special spicy drink. She mixes 4 pints of tomato juice and 4 pints of hot sauce. How many quarts or gallons did it make? _____

4. The fancy blue dress with sequins Martha bought at the mall was heavy. With all the sequins, it weighed 32 oz. How many grams was that? Remember, 453.59 grams equals 1 lb. _____

5. The mall was 17 kilometers from Martha's home. About how far is that in miles? One kilometer equals about ⅗ of a mile. _____

Crazy About Geometry

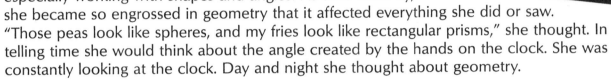

Sabrina Alexander, a geometry teacher at Hickock High School, loved her job. She loved everything about geometry, especially working with shapes and angles. As time went by, she became so engrossed in geometry that it affected everything she did or saw. "Those peas look like spheres, and my fries look like rectangular prisms," she thought. In telling time she would think about the angle created by the hands on the clock. She was constantly looking at the clock. Day and night she thought about geometry.

"We've got to help Sabrina out of this terrible obsession with geometry," said her friend Karen in the faculty lounge. "She spends her evenings reading geometry textbooks and measuring angles around her small apartment."

"What can we do to help her?" asked Carl sadly. "I tried to ask her out, but she turned me down so she could go downtown and check out shapes on the city hall building. I said I would go with her, but she said that I would be too much of a distraction. That was enough of a put-down for me," said Carl, a trigonometry teacher.

Karen was walking by Sabrina's classroom the next week when she heard a loud shriek. "What do you mean you didn't do your homework, Zachary? This is the fifth day in a row," Sabrina yelled out of control. "I can't stand it anymore. I can't stand it. I can't stand it," she kept mumbling until she collapsed into her chair as the bell rang for the end of the day.

Karen ran into the classroom, past the students who were scurrying out into the hall as fast as they could go. "She flipped out," said one student to Carl who was across the hall. Carl ran to get help.

"You need a long rest," said the psychiatrist to Sabrina. "Is there some place you have always wanted to go, but never had the time?" he asked. "You need to get as far away from your classroom as possible until you recover."

"Karen," said Sabrina. "You'll never guess where I'm going on vacation. Egypt!"

1. The Great Pyramid of Egypt was built of huge blocks of stone, each stone weighing 2½ tons. One ton is equal to 2,000 lbs. About how much did each stone weigh in kilograms? _____

2. Sabrina's favorite dress was black with pink polka dots. The diameter of the dots was 2 cm. What was the circumference of the pink polka dots?

   _____

3. It took Carl 3 minutes to get from Sabrina's classroom to the nearest phone to call for help. It took the rescue squad 3½ times longer to get to the Hickock High School. How long did it take the rescue squad to get to the school? _____

4. The psychiatrist charged Sabrina $120 per hour. Her insurance paid 80% of the cost of the sessions. How much did Sabrina end up paying per session? _____

5. Sabrina visited the pyramids at Giza. In all it had taken her 4 days of traveling to get to this point. The temperature was 98 degrees Fahrenheit. What was the temperature using the Celsius scale?

   _____

6. In 1339 B.C. Tutankhamen's mummy was placed into his hidden underground tomb. In 1922 Howard Carter found the burial chamber. How many years were there between the time the mummy was placed into the chamber and when it was discovered? _____

The Weirdest Emergency

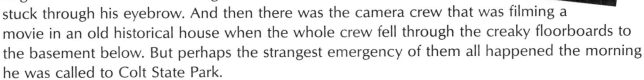

Freddie Farfaknuckle had been involved in some pretty weird emergencies, such as the Portuguese fisherman who had a huge hook attached to a fishing line and rod that was stuck through his eyebrow. And then there was the camera crew that was filming a movie in an old historical house when the whole crew fell through the creaky floorboards to the basement below. But perhaps the strangest emergency of them all happened the morning he was called to Colt State Park.

Janet and Manny had taken their children and pets to Colt State Park for a long, long five-day holiday weekend. Early on Saturday morning, the family dog Putter began chasing Sox the family cat around the campsite. Sox finally got tired of running, so he ran up the tree that he was afraid to come down. In fact, after unsuccessfully trying to coax Sox down for about three hours, the children convinced their dad to climb the tree and rescue Sox.

When he reached the fork in the tree where Sox was waiting, he reached up to grab the cat. But Sox was just beyond his reach. Manny tried to stretch just a bit higher by getting up on his tiptoes, but in doing so, lost his footing and fell. The good news was that his right leg fell through another fork in the tree and probably saved him from falling all the way to the ground. The bad news was that his right leg got stuck in the fork of the tree. He tried everything he could think of to free his leg, but with no success. Manny was also in pain from the fall. His daughter Betsy dialed 911 and Freddie Farfaknuckle answered the call.

When Freddie reached the campsite, he knew he had his work cut out for him! Not only did he have a big climb in front of him, but he also would still have Sox to deal with once he had freed Manny. So he used his tallest ladder to get to the main fork in the tree. His next move was to climb back down to where Manny was stuck. He then used his trusty saw to cut off the limb that would free Manny's leg. With this task completed, he helped Manny to the ladder, then proceeded on up the tree to get Sox.

When everyone (including Sox) was thankful to be back down on the ground, Freddie headed back to his truck, chuckling to himself. "I believe that's the weirdest rescue I've ever handled!"

1. The fire stations in Bristol each hold a different number of fire trucks. Along two intersecting streets there are a total of 5 fire stations with 1, 2, 3, 4, and 5 trucks in the different stations. Along each street the total number of trucks is the same. For example, if there are fire stations with a total of 12 trucks on Milk Street, then there are a total of 12 trucks in stations on Hope Street. Find and record as many answers for the locations of the fire trucks as possible.

    1, 2, 3, 4, and 5 trucks in different fire stations

    _____

2. Freddie enjoyed cooking for the other volunteers at the station. He decided to use a recipe that he must double to have enough. Rewrite the recipe so that it will feed 12 hungry people, instead of 6.

½ lb. of ground beef	3 ½ tsp. of chili powder
3- 32 oz. cans of kidney beans	⅛ tsp. of salt
¼ C. of chopped onions	⅔ tsp. of garlic powder
1 can of stewed tomatoes	1- 6 oz. can of tomato paste

    _____

    _____

    _____

    _____

3. The doubled recipe calls for 6- 32 oz. cans of kidney beans, but the fire station pantry has only 48 oz. cans. How many large cans of kidney beans should Freddie use? _____

4. The volunteers at the station in Bristol like to play a card game called War. In this game the face cards are wild. When you lay down a face card, you get to take 5 cards from your opponent. What are the chances of getting a face card in the whole deck? _____

5. The price for camping at Colt State Park is $15.00 per day. Residents of Bristol get a discount of 20%. Janet and Manny are Bristolians. Figure out how much they will save in 5 days of camping by being residents of Bristol._____

Jacob Asternaut's Sleep Problem

Jacob Asternaut had a sleep problem that was getting very annoying to him. He would go to bed every night at about 9:00 P.M. and fall right to sleep. "I have no problem going to sleep," he told the doctor. "And I seem to sleep through the night, but I wake up exhausted. Then during the day I fall asleep at the drop of a hat. Yesterday I fell asleep at a stop sign, while driving to school. The driver behind me honked the horn until I woke up."

"It was embarrassing last week when I fell asleep on my desk during an algebra test. The bell woke me at the end of the class. You can imagine my grade on that test," he uttered.

"I think I know what your problem is, but let's do some tests at the Kelly Sleep Clinic," said the doctor. Then Jacob found himself at the sleep clinic lying on a comfortable couch, wearing a black mask, hooked up with wires to a series of machines. He fell asleep almost immediately.

Jacob's heart rate and temperature lowered, and his breathing and muscles relaxed. He went from light sleep to a deeper sleep where his blood pressure dropped even lower. Then Jacob fell into the deepest sleep, which in most people lasts only a few minutes. In Jacob's case it lasted 45 minutes. During that time he talked in his sleep, which sounded more like mumbling and grunting. The amazing thing was that without an alarm clock, Jacob slept till almost noon the next day.

Later that day Jacob talked to Dr. Kennedy. "What's wrong, Doc?" Jacob asked.

"I'll have to do more tests, but so far you are showing signs of narcolepsy, a mysterious sleep condition. I'll know more after an EEG test."

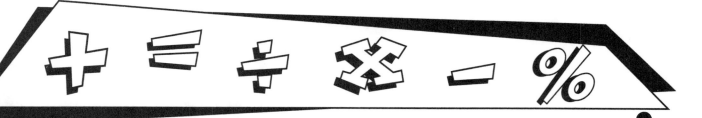

1. Elephants and giraffes only sleep for about 3 hours per night, while humans sleep about 8 hours per night. What is the fraction of the day that shows how long elephants and giraffes sleep? _____ Humans? _____

2. Bertha van der Merwe of South Africa once went without sleep for 11 days, 18 hours, and 55 minutes. How many minutes without sleep is this?

   _____

3. The last problem on Jacob's algebra test that he can remember answering was 5x - 3 = 32. Solve for x. _____

4. EEGs show that humans may be smarter than cats, but that we sleep alike. Cats sleep on an average of 18 hours per day, while humans sleep about 8 hours. If a cat and a human both fell asleep about 9:30 at night and slept straight through, what time would they wake up the next day? _____

5. Jacob received the bill from the sleep clinic about a month later. He gasped as he saw the bill for $2,700. His Blue Cross insurance would pay 80% of the bill. How much did Jacob's parents have to pay?

   _____

Easy Money

Colleen had a baby-sitting job Friday night, and she was looking forward to it. "I just have to take care of a seven-year-old boy from 7:00 to 12:00. That should be a breeze," she said to her boyfriend Scott. "I'll just let him watch TV till 8:00 and then put him to bed by 8:30. And the best part is I'll be making $5.50 an hour to talk on the phone."

Christopher's parents left with instructions about snacks and bedtime, and they left a phone number where they could be reached. For the first 20 minutes Christopher asked Colleen question after question in rapid fire motion. For the next hour, he yelled, jumped on furniture as though he were on a trampoline, poked and pulled Colleen's hair, and tried to drown out the sound of the TV with screams. "I'll have to call you back after I put the 'brat' to bed at 8:30," yelled Colleen to Scott.

"In your dreams," retorted Christopher. "I'm not tired. You can't make me go to bed," said Christopher as he jumped from the couch to the stuffed chair, and back again. Colleen chased Christopher through the house, as he ran from the living room, through the dining room, ending up in his parents' bedroom on their queen size bed.

"It's no use. I give up," resigned Colleen. "Do what you want because you will anyway."

At 11:45 Christopher's parents quietly opened the door to their house to find Colleen asleep on the couch and Christopher sleeping peacefully in his room. "I guess they did all right while we were gone," sighed Mrs. Graves with relief. "Colleen is the first baby sitter who didn't call in a panic for us to come home early. We'll have to call her again."

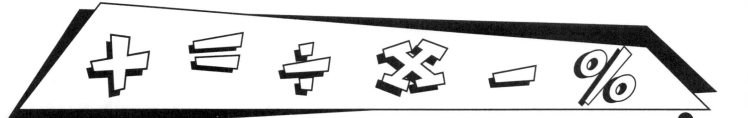

1. Colleen's age could be described as 2x - 3 = 29 with x being Colleen's age. What is Colleen's age? _____

2. How much money did Colleen make baby-sitting Christopher from 7:00 to 12:00? _____

3. Christopher had been through a lot of baby sitters before Colleen. His parents had to pay double the going rate for a baby sitter to attract someone to stay, so they could go out for some peace and quiet. What was the going rate for a baby sitter in that area?_____

4. Colleen had thought about calling Mr. and Mrs. Graves, but Christopher had torn off the last 2 digits of the phone number. This is what it looked like: 555-17. Colleen remembered that the last two digits added together equaled 8, and the last two digits multiplied together equaled 15. What were the last 2 digits? _____

5. Colleen decided to spend what she made baby-sitting on a sweater for $29.50 and a bottle of perfume for $19.00. How many more hours would she have to baby-sit Christopher to make enough money for the sweater and perfume? _____

Cloud Watching

It all started on a beautiful May morning in a secluded valley in western Virginia. Duncan Dustworthy, a dairy farmer with 54 black and white cows, was sitting on a stack of hay, chewing a piece of straw, and gazing at the clouds. The clouds were moving fast. They had formed thunderheads, and the clouds almost seemed to touch the ground.

Duncan was a lazy farmer. He hated to bring in the cows for milking, so he sent his trusted dog Chipper out to bring in the herd, while he sat around looking at the clouds. The weather looked bad that morning. The cows had already been milked and were slowly returning to the pasture. Duncan knew he should be working, but the work could wait.

Suddenly, the wind picked up whipping around the old broken down barn, pulling off the large front door which had been hanging by a hinge. Duncan's dog Chipper came running back from the pasture cowering in fear. "It's all right," consoled Duncan. "It's just a bad storm heading this way. No need to get excited."

Just then Duncan looked over to the West. There in the valley behind some trees was the largest tornado Duncan had ever seen. "Holy cow!" he shrieked at Chipper. "Get under the house," he screamed as he squeezed through the crawl space under the house.

As the tornado hit the cow pasture, he saw cows twirling as if they were on a carousel. Then he saw his herd of cows being thrown one by one out over the barn. In a flash even the barn was caught up in the whirling funnel cloud. Then it was gone, just as quickly as it had started. Everything but his house was gone. No more cows. No more barn. Even his old 1957 blue pickup truck was gone. Duncan, sitting on his front porch later that day, patted Chipper and went back to daydreaming and looking at the clouds.

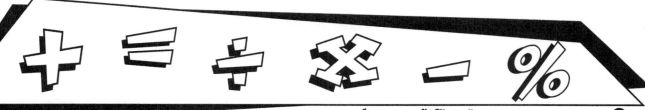

1. Duncan kept putting off milking the cows in the early morning. On Monday he milked the cows at 5:30. On Tuesday he milked the cows at 5:47, and on Wednesday he milked the cows at 6:04. If he continues in this pattern, what time would he have milked the cows on Thursday?

_____

2. Every spring Duncan's cows have babies. He keeps the cows and sells the bulls. Of the 54 babies, ⅔ of them were bulls. How many bulls is that? _____ What fraction of the babies were cows? _____

3. Duncan can sell the bulls for $47 each. How much will he make? _____ How many cows will he have now in his herd? _____

4. After the tornado, Duncan was making a list of his losses for the insurance company. The barn was valued at $2,050, the blue pickup truck at $430, and each cow was worth $225. Remember, he lost 54 cows. What is the total loss that Duncan will turn in to the insurance company? _____

5. Chipper ran out to the pasture after the tornado, looking for the cows. He ran back to the house, then back to the pasture, finally returning to Duncan who was sitting on the porch. The distance from the porch to the pasture is 1,320 feet. What is the total distance that Chipper ran in his wild frenzy after the tornado? _____

Cookie on a Cattle Drive

Jasper Adams was a cowboy who worked as a cookie on a cattle drive. A cookie's job was to drive the chuck wagon, a kitchen on wheels. Jasper fixed meals, tended wounds, cut hair, and sewed on buttons. He was a jack of all trades on a cattle drive.

The drive had had left south Texas heading to Abilene, Kansas, where the cattle would then be loaded onto trains for shipment to market. It had been a smooth crossing, and Jasper was anxious to get to Abilene. "What is this?" asked Jake tilting his hat back and scratching his head.

"It's 'son-of-a-gun' stew," uttered Jasper. "You know, you just throw the whole critter in the pot, except the hair and horns. You add hot sauce and cook for three hours."

"That's okay, but what kind of critter did you use?" asked Jake.

"It was a skunk," mentioned Jasper casually.

"A what?"

"You heard me," said Jasper. "A white-striped large smelly skunk."

"Okay," uttered Jake. No one argued with the cookie on the cattle drive.

Finally, the day came when they drove the last Texas Longhorn into the stockyards of Abilene. Now the fun began. "Jake, do you want to go into town to buy some new fancy duds? This is where we get paid. I'm not into yelling, shooting guns in the air, or visiting the saloons," said Jasper.

"Sounds good," said Jake excitedly. "As long as we stop for a large juicy steak and a cool drink. No offense," offered Jake, "But I'm tired of eating skunk, possum, and slimy rattlesnake."

"No offense taken," retorted Jasper. "As long as you're paying for supper."

1. "Son-of-a-gun" stew takes 4 hours to cook over an open fire on the range. Jasper started the stew when they stopped for the day at 6:45. At what time was the stew ready? _____

2. Jasper wore a wide-brimmed felt 10-gallon hat. Jake's hat was only a 6-gallon hat. The large pot for the stew held 32 quarts of water. How much larger was Jasper's hat than Jake's? _____ Whose hat could be used to bring water from the river in only one trip? _____

3. As cookie of the cattle drive, Jasper was given a bonus for his hard work. He received 18% more than Jake's pay of $12. How much did Jasper make? _____

4. In town Jasper and Jake went shopping at the General Store. Jasper bought a new set of chaps to protect his legs and a pair of shiny silver spurs with a revolving star at the back. He spent $7.26 on all his purchases. Jake spent all his money on a new saddle. Jasper agreed to loan Jake $3.00 at an interest rate of 1.5%. How much did Jake have to pay Jasper back on the loan of $3.00 with interest? _____

5. Jake was so happy that he decided to pay for supper. They stopped at the Golden Corral for a big juicy steak. The steaks here were so big that they decided to share a porterhouse steak weighing 16 oz. The steak was $.08 per ounce, and the baked potatoes were 2 for $.27. How much was the bill for supper? _____

Harry's Hair Dilemma

Harry was your average guy—not too wide and not too tall, not too fat and not too thin, not too rich and not too poor, not too smart and not too dumb, not too good at football and not too bad at soccer. Harry, however, continued to face a terrible dilemma. Each and every morning and each and every evening, Harry discovered, as he readied himself for the day or for bed, that he was losing hair. Lots and lots of hair! "What in the world am I going to do?" Harry lamented.

"Honey, I will love you no matter what!" Harry's wife Gina quickly assured him on more than one occasion. "Plenty of men lose their hair," comforted Gina, "and still go on to lead successful lives."

Harry knew that his wife was right but Harry did not care. He did not want to be BALD! Harry fretted and fretted and fretted. "Here I am only 28 years old, with a beautiful wife and two darling children, at the very peak of my career and balding!" Harry wailed.

Harry was so upset that he could hardly reason what to do next. His mother noticed the change in her only son and decided to broach the sensitive subject with her beloved. "Harry, do you remember your father before his untimely death?" Harry's mother questioned.

"Of course, I remember Dad," Harry looked despondent.

"Think back," encouraged Harry's mom. "Your father began to lose his hair when he too was a young man, Harry."

"But that can't be!" Harry seemed dubious.

"Oh yes," Mrs. Antonnuci chuckled. "Your father just had the good sense and the wisdom to enlist the services of Dr. Sparks in town."

"Who is Dr. Sparks?" questioned Harry. "What can anybody do about something like my hair? There's just none left for anybody to work with!" wailed Harry.

"Do you mean that you never heard your father speak of 'Regain'?" quizzed Harry's mother.

"Never heard of such a thing!" remarked a thoughtful Harry.

"Well, I certainly have marvelous news for you, Son!" exclaimed Mrs. Antonnuci. "One application of Regain and I can assure you if my memory serves me well, you will be on your way to a new and happier you!" stated Harry's mom.

Harry could hardly wait for the day of his scheduled appointment with Dr. Sparks. Finally, with great anticipation a nervous and yet excited Harry walked through the doors of Dr. Sparks' clinic. After a brief and informal introduction and examination, Dr. Sparks informed an anxious and apprehensive Harry that he had approximately 100 hair follicles per square inch as opposed to a normal person's 500 hair follicles per square inch. Harry sadly learned that his balding area measured ten square inches.

Dr. Sparks assured Harry that he would have a full head of bushy, curly hair within a reasonable amount of time. In fact, he assured Harry that if he followed the prescribed applications, Harry could anticipate hair growth at the rate of a five percent increase per month.

1. What are the total number of hairs in Harry's balding area? _____

2. How many hairs would be in this same area on a normal head of hair? _____

3. What percent less hair does Harry have than a normal person would have?_____

4. At the rate of 5%, how long should it take Harry to cultivate a full head of bushy, curly hair? _____

5. If "Regain" costs $42.50 per 10-oz. bottle and each bottle contains a one-month supply of applications, how much will it cost Harry to become hairy? _____

6. If Harry becomes tired of using this treatment and discontinues use after one year, how much money will Harry have spent? _____

7. How many hairs could Harry expect to have if he discontinued use of the treatment after one year? _____

Spreading the News

Alice rushed to the mailbox one cold and cloudy afternoon in February to get the mail before her troublesome brother Joe arrived home from school and beat her to the punch. Alice absolutely loved to retrieve the mail before any other family members. Maybe it was because Alice felt that this was one of the few things that she could do first in a family of ten. With five sisters and three brothers, Alice was never first to do anything!

Alice threw her coat on the kitchen chair and sorted through the bills, the advertisements, the brochures, the magazines, and the letters. "Aah, just what I have been waiting for!" Alice commented out loud. The letter from the Clearing Barn Sweepstakes was Alice's chance for fame, fortune, and riches. Alice could hardly contain her excitement as she read and reread the registered letter that had arrived. The letter informed Alice Pennywise that she was the lucky winner of the $10,000 sweepstakes she had entered!

A gleeful Alice could not wait to spread the news far and wide to any and everyone who cared to listen about her incredible good fortune. An elated Alice grabbed the phone to call three of her closest friends to spread her good news. "You are never going to believe what has just this very minute happened to me," Alice casually commented to her next-door neighbor. Alice could not wait to tell her very best friend Leigh Anne all about her good fortune, and before the hour was out Alice had telephoned her steady boyfriend. "Gary, do I have some unbelievable news to share with you," Alice screamed excitedly into the phone. The very next day, each of Alice's excited friends called three of their friends to tell them all about Alice's good news. Can you believe that the next day those three friends called three friends of their own to spread Alice's good news all about the Clearing Barn Sweepstakes?

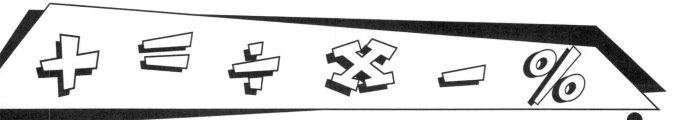

1. If Alice's three closest friends continued this pattern throughout the remainder of the week, how many people were contacted by phone about Alice's good news by the seventh day? _____

Alice, in her initial excitement, told each of her brothers and sisters about her win in the sweepstakes. Each brother and sister in turn called 2 of their friends to spread their sister's good news. Each of those 2 friends in turn called 3 of their friends to explain about Alice's good luck. Each of these 3 friends called 4 of their friends to explain about Alice's good fortune.

2. How many people now know about Alice's win in the Clearing Barn Sweepstakes? _____

The town newspaper, *The Gossip*, that boasted a circulation of 5,000 customers printed Alice's good news on Sunday in the "Daily Break." Statistics continue to indicate that 20% of the subscribers read only the front page, the comics, "Dear Hillary," and the "Daily Break."

3. How many people (which includes her 3 friends and their friends, the brothers and sisters, and the newspaper) to date have heard about Alice and her mail about the sweepstakes winnings? _____

Ida Mae and the College Fund

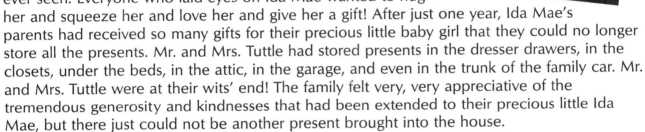

Ida Mae was the cutest and the cuddliest little baby that you have ever seen. Everyone who laid eyes on Ida Mae wanted to hug her and squeeze her and love her and give her a gift! After just one year, Ida Mae's parents had received so many gifts for their precious little baby girl that they could no longer store all the presents. Mr. and Mrs. Tuttle had stored presents in the dresser drawers, in the closets, under the beds, in the attic, in the garage, and even in the trunk of the family car. Mr. and Mrs. Tuttle were at their wits' end! The family felt very, very appreciative of the tremendous generosity and kindnesses that had been extended to their precious little Ida Mae, but there just could not be another present brought into the house.

The Tuttles faced not only the dilemma about where to store the wealth of Ida Mae's baby gifts but also what in the world were the Tuttles to buy their own daughter on her first birthday. "Let's surprise Ida Mae with a beautiful pink tricycle that she could ride as she gets older!" Mrs. Tuttle suggested.

"Where do you think that we could store that beautiful pink tricycle until Ida Mae is old enough to ride it?" asked Mr. Tuttle.

"You are right, Dear," lamented Mrs. Tuttle. "I've got it!" Mrs. Tuttle exclaimed gleely. "We can buy Ida Mae a pony we can board at Creek Bed Stables!" Mrs. Tuttle stated excitedly.

"Dot Tuttle, what in the world has come over you?" questioned Mr. Tuttle. "Do you really think we should pay to board a pony until Ida Mae is old enough to ride this horse?"

"Oh, I guess you are right again," responded Mrs. Tuttle sadly.

Ida Mae's parents thought and thought and thought and finally a terrific idea came to them. "It is perfect!" exclaimed Mrs. Tuttle. "Our idea won't require any storage and it certainly will benefit her future," cooed Mrs. Tuttle. "We can establish a college fund for our precious one-year-old Ida Mae! I'm sure that our baby girl will need lots of money for an education when the time comes because Ida Mae is destined to become somebody very, very special!" said Mrs. Tuttle lovingly.

"Yeah," replied Mr. Tuttle. "I am already quite sure that my baby girl will be a lawyer, a doctor, an architect, or even an actress with her good looks and her winning personality. Ida Mae might even be the first woman president," beamed Mr. Tuttle.

On Ida Mae's first birthday the Tuttles opened a special account in Ida Mae's name to be used solely for her college education. The Tuttles made an initial deposit of 50¢. Ida Mae's parents agreed to double the deposit each year up to and including Ida Mae's seventeenth birthday.

1. How much money will Ida Mae have in her account on her second birthday? _____

2. How much money will Ida Mae have in her account on her tenth birthday? _____

3. How much money will Ida Mae have in her account on her eighteenth birthday? _____

When Ida Mae turned 18, she was accepted at 3 colleges with tuitions ranging from $8,593.00 to $14,991.00 to $18,500.00 per year. Ida Mae liked all three schools equally, so their cost was not a factor in her decision.

4. Does Ida Mae have enough money that has accumulated in her college fund to attend each of the 3 colleges for 4 years? _____

5. If the second university (that costs $14,991.00 per year) offers Ida Mae a $2,000.00 scholarship, and the third college (that costs $18,500.00 per year) offers Ida Mae a $9,000.00 scholarship, which schools can Ida Mae attend? _____

Sneak Previews

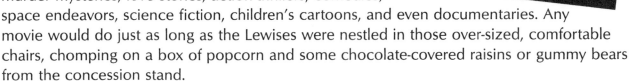

Leslie and Ashton Lewis had always been avid movie goers who had dreamed of opening their very own movie theater. The Lewises loved to watch murder mysteries, love stories, action-thrillers, comedies, space endeavors, science fiction, children's cartoons, and even documentaries. Any movie would do just as long as the Lewises were nestled in those over-sized, comfortable chairs, chomping on a box of popcorn and some chocolate-covered raisins or gummy bears from the concession stand.

Not a single day passed that Leslie did not think of another scheme to finance such a tremendously expensive undertaking as opening a movie theater. "What if we went to that bank down on Twenty-first Street for a business loan?" Leslie asked.

"The interest rate on such a loan would eat us alive! That's a ridiculous idea!" Ashton exclaimed.

"What if we borrowed the money for a down payment from my family?" Leslie tried again.

"You know the old saying that families and money do not mix," Ashton retorted. So year after year went by while the Lewises continued to save one tenth of their weekly salaries.

Surprisingly, one bright and sunny Friday afternoon Leslie received a monthly bank statement in the mail and was overwhelmed to realize that enough money had accumulated in a relatively short amount of time to finance their business. The adventurous duo chatted at dinner and excitedly decided to take the plunge and open their very own movie theater in New Buck County, Alabama.

The new construction took six months to complete but houses eight separate large screen theaters with maximum seating capacities of 250 seats per theater. Leslie and Ashton were really excited when on opening night 744 people attended the sneak preview showings for the 7:00 shows. Can you believe that at 10:00 1,016 people attended the late night sneak previews?

1. What is the total number of seats available in the theater? _____

2. If the 744 people attending the 7:00 sneak preview were evenly distributed in the 8 theaters, how many people would have been in each show? _____

3. If the 1,016 people attending the 10:00 performance were evenly divided among the 8 theaters, how many people would be in each theater? __

4. Find the number of people in the theater if 32 people attended the murder mystery, 172 attended the children's cartoon, 13 attended the science-fiction movie, 233 attended the action thriller, 98 attended the comedy, 14 attended the love story, 71 attended the documentary, and 22 attended the space endeavor.

   _____

5. If each theater must have a 50% attendance rate to make a profit, how many theaters made a profit? _____

6. List at least 3 variables that might have affected the attendance of the most popular movie. _____

7. If the Lewises charged $6.25 per ticket, how much money did the owners take in on opening night?_____

The Daytuna 500 Race

Sammy Spark Plug and Frankie Fast had been friends for years. The boys had first met at the Daytuna 500 race in Daytuna Beach, Florida, nearly 25 years before. Sammy had been the pit manager, and Frankie had been a driver at the most prestigious Fascar races of the year. Today felt just like old times. "Now this race track has been extended and is positively five miles in length," yelled Sammy from the pit as Frankie prepared to climb into his machine. "You know that your car can travel an average of 200 miles per hour and has a 40-gallon gas tank," Sammy shouted above a crowd of more than 10,000 spectators.

"You of all people know that I am very familiar with all the statistics on my car," responded Frankie Fast. "Remember, Boss," cried Frankie, "I am the undefeated champion of the Daytuna 500!"

"Be ready after the next lap to come on in," radioed Sammy to Frankie. "You know the Fascar policy," stated Sammy over the two-way radio. "It has been 400 miles and those tires on your machine have got to be changed."

Frankie Fast has been on the track for one hour and seventeen minutes. Sammy Spark and the pit crew have been up all night preparing Frankie's car for the big event. Sammy and the crew need some sandwiches and some drinks to keep them going, "I'll go for the food," volunteered one of the crew.

"Let me!" offered another. "I'm ready for a break."

"I have been in that pit longer than all of you fellows and I am going," Sammy volunteered decisively. "I anticipate that it will take me approximately 22 minutes at the Greasy Spoon to get the burgers and drinks. I am going to make my own run and I will be back in a flash!" Sammy assured the weary workers.

1. How long will it take Frankie Fast to make one lap around the track? __

2. How many laps around the race track did Frankie Fast make before the tires on his car had to be changed? _____

3. How much time will elapse before Frankie Fast needs his tires changed again? _____ Will Sammy have enough time to purchase the refreshments for himself and the pit crew? _____

4. If Frankie's car's average fuel consumption is 5 miles per gallon during the race, how many times can Frankie go around the track on one tank of gas? _____

5. How much time does Sammy Spark have to purchase the food and get back to the pit before Frankie Fast will need more gas? _____

6. If the Daytuna 500 race lasts for 4 hours, what is the total amount of gas that will be consumed? _____

One Hundred Hungry Ants

It would appear to the ignorANT
as well as to the observANT that ants are merely annoying insects,
not in the least a concern or a threat to the casual picnicker. JubilANT and RadiANT,
however, were brilliANT, not defiANT ants with unpleasANT attitudes, but ants with a
fANTastic scheme! The two brothers had devised a plan to raid a picnic and eat until
they and the members of their colony could hold no more. "I have used my ANTennae
and found the perfect location for a giANT raid!" an elated JubilANT shared with
BrilliANT. "Just ten feet south of this very spot there is an unsuspecting couple with an
infANT intent on devouring four hot dogs each weighing 1.6 ounces, four hot dog buns
each weighing 1.0 ounces, two apples each weighing 4.0 ounces and one gigANTic
piece of cake weighing five ounces. I have seen it with my very own eyes!" an
observANT JubilANT squealed with anticipation. "Our mission is to be patient and lay in
wait."

"I won't throw a tANTrum even though that is quite a walk," promised BrilliANT.
JubilANT and BrilliANT assembled the remaining 98 members of their colony at 11:00
sharp and set out upon their quest.

Upon arrival at the campsite some 36 minutes after departure, JubilANT and BrilliANT
immediately analyzed the situation. BrilliANT reasoned, "Each of us weighs .01 ounces
and each member of our colony can eat five times its weight."

"Each ant can carry ten times its own weight," JubilANT added. "Let's send a scout with
a cANTeen to survey the site one more time. We need to know how many trips it is
going to take us to move the picnickers' food to our location so we can eat in peace!"

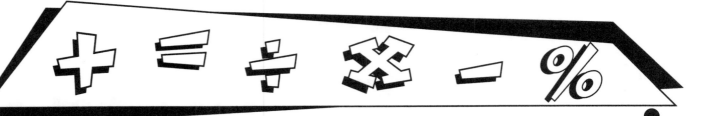

1. Can 100 hungry ants carry all the hot dogs in one trip?

   _____

2. How many ants will it take to accomplish this task? _____

3. How many ants will it take to carry the hot dog buns to the colony?

   _____

4. Can 100 ants carry 2 apples and 1 piece of delicious cake in 1 trip?

   _____

5. If the 100 hungry ants cannot carry the 2 apples and 1 piece of cake in one trip, how many ants would it take to move the food?

   _____

After the colony of ants carried the food back to their location, a new discovery is made. "We can't possibly eat all of these delectable delights in one sitting!" exclaimed BrilliANT.

"You're right! This feast is just too much for even 100 hungry ants to eat in one day!" lamented a greedy JubilANT.

6. How many ounces of food will be left over after the feast of the 100 hungry ants? _____

7. Approximately how many days will it take the ants to consume all of the food? _____

Rocky's Roads

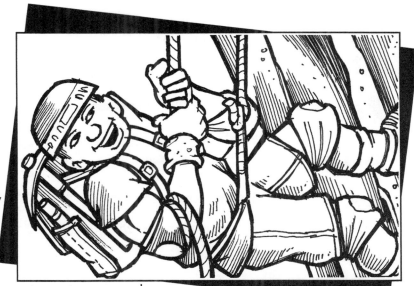

Rocky Top was a mountain climber who absolutely craved excitement and adventure. Rocky was bored to tears at the mundane and monotonous perils of everyday existence, so Rocky was continually planning his next thrill. No mountain was too steep, too rugged, or too treacherous for Rocky! The thrill of the unexpected and the unbelievable as well as the thrill of danger were uppermost in Rocky's subconscious mind. Rarely was there a day that passed that Rocky did not fantasize about his next big climb.

One day, after years of wishful daydreaming about the "Big Climb," Rocky decided to take the plunge. "I am quitting my job of $52,000.00 per year," he calmly explained to his boss. "I've divorced my wife of 22 years. I took my two pet dogs to the kennel, sold my car, cashed in my retirement, canceled my life-insurance policies, and withdrew my savings from the local bank," Rocky matter-of-factly continued to explain. "At long last Rocky Top is free to pursue his dream!" an elated Rocky shared with his past employer.

Rocky rushed to his local travel agent. "Give me a ticket that will take me to the frontiers of Tibet and Nepal and the adventure of a lifetime!" The ticket agent looked confused. An exuberant Rocky joyfully elaborated to the girl at the counter, "I'm on my way to climb Rocky Top, one of the highest mountains in the entire world!"

"You can do that all by yourself?" the confused young woman questioned Rocky.

"Gosh, I guess I really didn't even think about the details such as supplies or guides," an alarmed Rocky revealed, "but I have an entire lifetime to plan a trip of this magnitude. I'm up to the challenge!" a confident Rocky rebounded.

Upon landing, the very first thing Rocky did was to hire an interpreter, a guide, and a mountain porter to help with the tremendous and awesome task of scaling the world's tallest mountain. "Mountain porters can be expected to carry an average of 100 pounds of supplies on their backs," the guide explained to Rocky. "I have calculated that our party will need 1,200 pounds of supplies transported from Base Camp #1 that is presently located at an altitude of 2,000 feet above sea level to Base Camp #2 that is presently located at an altitude of 5,000 feet above sea level," explained the interpreter and the guide to the novice Rocky. "Also," continued the guide, "we need to remember in our calculations that mountain porters will only be able to carry 80 percent of their normal loads when transporting supplies from Base Camp #1 to Base Camp #2 and 60 percent of their normal loads when transporting supplies from Base Camp #2 to Base Camp #3."

Rocky quickly assessed, "I guess a good rule of thumb would be to say that the higher the altitude the thinner the air and the greater the reduction in carrying capacity."

1. How many mountain porters will be required to carry the supplies to Base Camp #2? _____

2. How many fewer mountain porters would be needed to carry the supplies to Base Camp #2 if thinning altitude was not a factor?

   _____

After an uneventful trip from Base Camp #1 to Base Camp #2, Rocky's party of guides, interpreters, and mountain porters agreed to stop at Base Camp #2 for several days to rest and repack their gear for the additional climb to Base Camp #3 at an elevation of 10,000 feet above sea level—the top. The guides reported that they anticipated the party would consume 200 pounds of the supplies and would leave behind 400 pounds of used supplies.

3. If the party consumes 200 pounds of supplies and leaves behind another 400 pounds of equipment before they begin the final climb to the top, how many mountain porters will be needed to carry the remainder of supplies to Base Camp #3? _____

4. If the atmosphere is not a factor, how many mountain porters would be needed to transport the supplies to Base Camp #3? _____

5. If Rocky has to leave 10 porters at Base Camp #2, how many porters should Rocky initially hire to ensure that he has enough men to carry the supplies to Base Camp #3? _____

Some-thing's Fishy

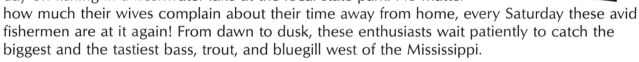

Charlie A. Tuna, Tony T. Trout, and Sammy A. Salmon have been friends for years. Every Saturday these friends spend their day off fishing in a freshwater lake at the local state park. No matter how much their wives complain about their time away from home, every Saturday these avid fishermen are at it again! From dawn to dusk, these enthusiasts wait patiently to catch the biggest and the tastiest bass, trout, and bluegill west of the Mississippi.

"I don't even like the sight of a fish much less the taste of fish anymore!" exclaimed Tony Trout's wife.

"I have put my foot down and warned Sammy that not another fish is to be put in that freezer," threatened Sammy Salmon's upset wife.

"Exactly how much is this habit of theirs costing us?" inquired Charlie's disgruntled wife. "I just read in the local newspaper that the game warden imposes a tax of 50¢ per pound on any fish caught!"

"Tony tells me that the guys are careful to follow the state laws requiring that they throw back any fish they catch over the set limits," added Mrs. Trout.

"I know, I know! But the fellows use minnows and worms for bait that they purchase at the tackle shop each week, and the average weight of a bass is two pounds, the average weight of a trout is one pound and the average weight of a bluegill is one-half pound," exclaimed Charlie's wife. "You both have seen the weekly supply of bass, trout, and bluegills they bring home. It's got to be costing us a small fortune!"

"What are the limits, and exactly how many fish are the guys bringing home each week?" questioned an unknowing Mrs. Trout.

"Sammy tells me that the game warden enforces a limit of 10 bass, 15 trout, and 20 bluegill per fisherman per day," Mrs. Salmon reported.

"This shouldn't be hard to figure," calculated Mrs. Tuna. "Charlie caught 9 bass, 9 trout, and 9 bluegill last week."

"Tony brought home 20 bass, 20 trout, and 20 bluegill," Mrs. Trout volunteered, "because I helped fillet the fish for our freezer."

"Sammy didn't get any bass last week, but he did catch 9 trout and 9 bluegill," reported Mrs. Salmon.

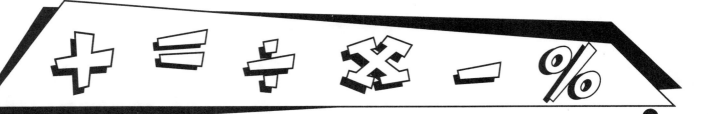

1. If Charlie A. Tuna caught 9 bass, 9 trout, and 9 bluegill, what percent of his total allowed daily limit did Charlie catch? _____

2. If Tony T. Trout caught 20 bass, 20 trout, and 20 bluegill, what percent of his total allowed daily limit did Tony bring home? _____

3. If Sammy A. Salmon caught 9 trout and 9 bluegill, what percent of his total allowed daily limit did Sammy catch? _____

4. What was the weight of the fish taken home by Charlie A. Tuna? _____

5. What was the weight of the fish taken home by Tony T. Trout? _____

6. What was the weight of the fish taken home by Sammy A. Salmon? _____

7. If the game warden collected a state park tax of 50¢ per pound for any fish caught, what was the combined amount of money Charlie, Tony, and Sammy had to pay last Saturday? _____

8. What was the average cost per fish after the state park tax was paid by the fishermen? _____

The Boring Trip

Mr. and Mrs. Boring and the two Boring children Pete and Repeat set out upon their yearly family vacation to visit the state of Wyoming. The family traveled for three days west on U.S. Highway 9 before boredom set in and the children began to complain. "When are we going to get there?" questioned Pete.

"How much longer?" asked Repeat.

"It will be a little longer children," replied Mrs. Boring as an 18-wheeler sped by the Boring utility vehicle. "Dad, that sign on the back of that truck says it pays $11,000.00 per year in taxes. How much do we pay in road taxes?" wondered Pete.

"I truthfully don't know how much we pay per year for road taxes," pondered Mr. Boring, "but I can tell you that we do pay $1.25 per gallon of gasoline and ⅖ of the cost of gasoline is mandated to be spent on road taxes."

"Our car averages 20 miles per gallon," interjected Mrs. Boring, "and we traveled 18,000 miles last year in this very car."

Mrs. Boring had a brilliant idea! "I'll entertain the children with road games before they begin to bicker," she thought to herself. "Children, let's conduct a survey for the next two hours of the most popular color car and the most traveled direction on Highway 9."

"Tally the most popular car color traveling east, Repeat, and I will determine the coolest car color traveling west," Pete quickly took the lead.

"Your mother didn't say the coolest car color, Pete. That's a matter of personal opinion," reported Mr. Boring. "She said the most popular car color traveling in your designated direction on U.S. Highway 9 in the next two hours. You can report only what you see, and you must report only the data that you find," concluded Mr. Boring. "We will discuss some of the variables that may affect the outcome later."

"While we are collecting this data, we can also determine whether the cars we are surveying have an in-state or out-of-state license plate," Repeat excitedly interjected.

"Children, you may begin!" Mr. Boring called everyone to attention.

1. How much money does the Boring family pay in road taxes a year? _____

2. After reviewing the results of Pete and Repeat's surveys below, determine what was the most popular color of car. _____

3. What percentage of the total number of cars surveyed does the most popular car color represent? _____

4. What was the least popular car color? _____ What percent of the total number of cars surveyed does the least popular car color represent? _____

5. What direction did the most number of cars travel? _____

6. What was the average number of cars traveling west? _____

7. What was the average number of cars traveling east? _____

8. Which child had the most number of cars to count in the 2-hour period? _____

Car Color and Direction Survey

	White	Red	Blue	Black	Silver
Pete	100	10	30	50	10
Repeat	70	5	20	50	5

Freddie's Fertilizer

Freddie Fescue and his lovely wife Bermudae have always lived in Florida on what Freddie considers a sizeable estate that measures 100 feet by 200 feet. Neighbors near and far continue to comment year after year that Freddie has the most beautiful lawn they have ever seen. No wonder! No matter the condition of the lawn, Freddie fertilizes that beautiful lawn season after season. Golf courses don't look as perfectly manicured as Freddie's lawn. Famous resorts in remote, hideaway places can't boast of the lush, green expanses that Freddie maintains right outside his front door. Freddie has often been known to comment, "This gorgeous lawn does not come without some financial restraints! I can't afford to continue this costly venture season after season. I'm broke!" lamented a financially strapped Freddie. "The cost of all this fertilizer is just too much. I'm going to have to begin to compare prices."

"A few quick calculations and some keen investigation into pricing should certainly improve my plight," a despondent Freddie thought. "My house measures 30 feet by 100 feet with a deck of 20 by 20 feet. My garage is detached and measures 20 feet by 25 feet with a driveway 10 feet wide and 100 feet long. Certainly I must not forget the necessary deductions from my square footage calculations for that brick sidewalk coming from my house that measures 4 feet by 25 feet," Freddie pondered.

"If I buy fertilizer and rent a spreader, maybe that will be the cheapest way to continue to fertilize my grass four times a year. Fertilizer costs $10.00 for a 5,000-square-foot bag, $15.00 for a 10,000-square-foot bag, or $20.00 for a 15,000-square-foot bag. The cost of a spreader is $20.00 a day, and I can certainly fertilize my yard in just one day," contemplated Freddie.

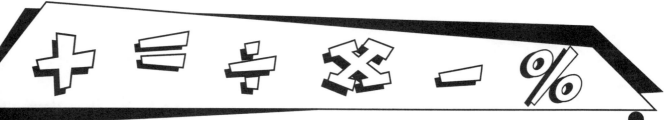

1. How many square feet of grass are in Freddie's lawn? _____

2. What is the most inexpensive way to purchase fertilizer?
_____

3. What will be the cost per year to purchase the most inexpensive
fertilizer and to rent the spreader?_____

"'Barefeet' Lawn Service provides wonderful maintenance for the Grub family lawn in the next block for only five cents per square foot," Freddie continued to think. "I just read in Sunday's newspaper that the company is running a special. I believe that first-time participants are eligible for a first-time deal of one cent per square foot. Second-, third-, and fourth-time participants will be charged five cents per square foot," Freddie recalled.

4. What will be the cost if Barefeet Lawn Service fertilizes Freddie's lawn?
_____

"I don't know! Maybe I should just hire that kid next door to do it all." Freddie continued to contemplate, "I hear that Billie Bob charges $50.00 each time he fertilizes unless the customer agrees to a yearly deal. Then, of course, rumor has it that Billie Bob will agree to give a 25% discount."

5. What will be the cost for Billie Bob to fertilize Freddie's lawn for one
year? _____

6. Which of the three choices is the most inexpensive option for Freddie to
use to have his yard fertilized? _____

7. What would be the most expensive option? _____

Cookies a Plenty

Mrs. Alfalfa Sprout is at it again! For the eighth year in a row, the girls' varsity cheerleader sponsor is busy organizing Cook County High School's trip to Dizzy World. The girls on the squad need to accumulate points by selling their delicious home-baked cookies. "Why, everyone knows the girls bake the best cookies this side of the Mississippi," Mrs. Sprout and her two children, Bean and Brussel, were quick to tell any novice in town who had not sampled the tasty treats.

"Each box of cookies is valued with a point value, and the girls have to earn a cumulative total of 700 points to pay for their expenses to the Magic Kingdom," Mrs. Sprout continued to explain to those present at the local town meeting. "I feel that it is so important now days that young people accept some of the responsibility for their costly adventures. With the support of good citizens such as yourself and with the girls' delicious efforts available for sale, my princesses are sure to raise enough points to send them on their way to Dizzy World again this year!"

"Marsha's cookies are marvelously moist, mouth-watering macaroons, masked with melted marshmallows and valued at five points a box. Stella's sinfully scrumptious, double-stuffed dooreos contain creamy vanilla sandwiched amid savory sweetened, chewy, chocolate wafers and are worth four points a box. Francis's fabulously flawless and fluffy devil's food cookies are fattening but yet fancy, fantastic, and doubtlessly drizzled with creamy marshmallows and rich chocolate to die for! These cookies are worthy of three points a box. Tina's turbulent, tantalizingly thick and tormentingly good cherries are tucked tightly within the deepest, darkest, and sweetest of chocolates and are valued at two points a box. Last but not least, Lucy's luscious, lemon lady fingers literally ladened with a little light meringue are valued at a point per box. Who in their right mind could possibly resist such an awesome selection of delectable delights?" Mrs. Sprout questioned in sheer wonder.

Three weeks later with sales completed, Mrs. Sprout happily announced the results of the cookie sales: "Marsha sold 5 boxes of mouth-watering macaroons,10 boxes of double-stuffed dooreos, 10 boxes of tantalizing chocolate cherry cookies, 15 boxes of lemon lady fingers, and 25 boxes of devil's food cookies. Francis can be credited with selling 10 boxes of dooreos and 10 boxes of delicious devil's food cookies as well as 5 boxes of macaroons, 5 boxes of chocolate cherries, and 5 boxes of lemon lady fingers. Lucy hasn't been so lucky because she has not sold the first box of macaroons and only 5 boxes of dooreos although she can be congratulated for selling 20 boxes of devil's food cookies, 10 boxes of chocolate cherries, and 15 boxes of lemon lady fingers. On the other hand, Tina appears to be our top seller with a record breaking 30 boxes of dynamite devil's food cookies, 20 boxes of macaroons, 5 boxes of dooreos, 5 boxes of chocolate cherry cookies, but not the first box of lemon lady fingers. Stella is to be commended for contributing points with her cookie sales of 10 boxes of dooreos, chocolate cherry, and lemon lady fingers; 5 boxes of macaroons; and 15 boxes of devil's food cookies. Each of you has done an absolutely marvelous job. I'm so proud of your efforts, girls!"

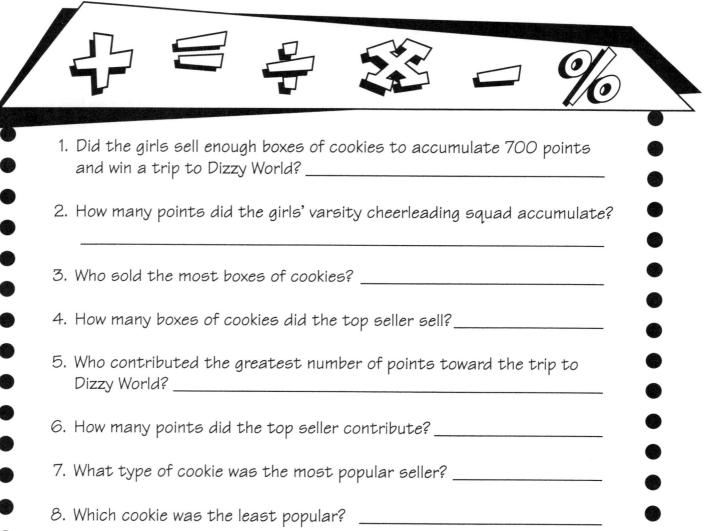

1. Did the girls sell enough boxes of cookies to accumulate 700 points and win a trip to Dizzy World? _____

2. How many points did the girls' varsity cheerleading squad accumulate? _____

3. Who sold the most boxes of cookies? _____

4. How many boxes of cookies did the top seller sell? _____

5. Who contributed the greatest number of points toward the trip to Dizzy World? _____

6. How many points did the top seller contribute? _____

7. What type of cookie was the most popular seller? _____

8. Which cookie was the least popular? _____

Nicole's Adventure

Nicole and her family spent their vacation at Fantasy World Amusement Park. The amusement park is so large that a train is used to assist people in traveling between attractions. The train conductor's name is Rudy. He is a creative and friendly train conductor and designed the train system used at Fantasy World Amusement Park.

The train makes stops in the following order: Main Station, Animal Kingdom, Future World, Old New York, Sports Center, Rain Forest, Transportation Hub, and Wild West Town. The train travels in a loop, so the next stop will be a return to Main Station.

The train conductor decided to let Nicole operate the train. He warned her that the train travels in two directions: forward and backward. If the train starts at Main Station and wants to travel forward to Future World, then the conductor presses +2. The positive sign means to travel forward, and the 2 indicates the number of stations that must be traveled. If the train starts at Sports Center and wants to travel to Future World, then the conductor presses -2. The negative sign means to travel backward, and the 2 indicates the number of stations that must be traveled.

The conductor told Nicole that there is one rule that she must follow very carefully. The method used to decide whether to travel forward or backward is based on the direction that represents the shortest distance.

Rudy gave Nicole a practice run of the train. The train began at Old New York and needed to travel to Main Station. Rudy asked Nicole, "Should the train travel forward or backward?"

Nicole remembered the rule about traveling the shortest route. She said, "We should travel backward three stations!"

The conductor was happy. He asked, "What should you press?" Nicole pressed -3 and the train traveled to the correct station.

At that moment the conductor was called to the office. He told Nicole that he trusted her math ability and that she must be the conductor until he returned. Nicole agreed.

See if you can select the correct number to press to direct the train. Nicole created a map of the park to help her find her way. You may wish to do the same.

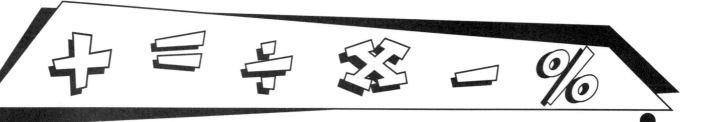

1. Try to guess the correct number to press to direct the train from the Main Station to each of the following:

   a. Wild West Town _____

   b. Future World _____

   c. Transportation Hub _____

   d. Old New York _____

2. Which station is the same distance from Main Station whether the train travels forward or backward? _____

The Tampa Experiment

Summer vacation from school in Tampa began with a rainy day for Jim and his friends, Shanita and Kelly. The three had met in Mr. Baker's math class and immediately formed a genuine friendship that all three felt would last a lifetime.

Shanita suggested that they start a business to raise money for a trip to the local water slide park in August. Jim and Kelly felt that this was a great idea and agreed to think of a business location that would earn the most money for the group.

The next day, the trio from Tampa met to consider each person's plan. Kelly thought that the group could sell fruit juice at the corner of Main Street and Juniper Avenue. The juice would cost them 5¢ a cup, and they could sell the juice for 25¢ a cup. Main Street is very heavily traveled, and the selected location has convenient parking for cars.

Shanita suggested that the group could sell candy bars at the intersection of First Street and Pacific Avenue. Each candy bar would cost the friends 15¢ and they could sell each bar for 25¢. First Street is very busy and has no parking for cars.

Jim came to the group with an idea to sell cookies at a location where Third Street meets Atlantic Avenue. Each pack of cookies would cost the group 20¢ and could be sold for 25¢. Third Street has very little traffic and plenty of parking.

The group wrote each suggestion on a chalkboard and began the process of deciding which plan would have the greatest potential for raising the most money for the group.

1. What factors should the group consider when selecting the best plan?

   _____

   _____

2. How much profit will there be from each fruit juice sold? _____
   Each candy bar sold? _____ Each cookie pack sold?
   _____

3. Assuming that 50 cars stop at each location, how much money would
   be raised if each car purchased one item at each location?

        fruit juice _____   cookie pack _____

        candy bar _____

4. Which plan would you recommend that the group explore? Explain your
   answer. _____

   _____

   _____

A Calculating Dilemma

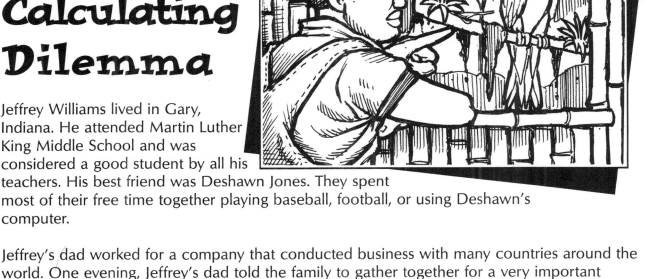

Jeffrey Williams lived in Gary, Indiana. He attended Martin Luther King Middle School and was considered a good student by all his teachers. His best friend was Deshawn Jones. They spent most of their free time together playing baseball, football, or using Deshawn's computer.

Jeffrey's dad worked for a company that conducted business with many countries around the world. One evening, Jeffrey's dad told the family to gather together for a very important meeting. He told them that his company wanted to send him to Costa Rica for two years. The company needed his expertise to help the government of Costa Rica save the rain forest and the animals living there. The company was willing to pay for the entire Williams' family to live with their dad in Costa Rica. The family had to vote on whether to go or not! Jeffrey did not want to leave Deshawn but felt that if his dad could help save the animals of the rain forest, then it was worth the trip. Anyway, he would be back to see Deshawn in two years. The family voted and all agreed to the move to Costa Rica.

Three months later, the family arrived in San Jose, Costa Rica. The company purchased a house for the Williams' family. The very first day that Jeffrey spent in his new country, he spotted white faced monkeys and red fronted amazon parrots. He could not believe the beauty of the rain forest and all of the creatures living there. He thought this would be a great place to spend the next two years.

Jeffrey's family planned a trip to the beach at Manual Antonio Park, which borders the Pacific Ocean. He turned on the radio to check the weather forecast. The forecast was great except for the predicted temperature. The forecaster said that the high for the day was to be 18 degrees! Jeffrey looked outside, and the breeze was warm and the palm trees had not frozen! Jeffrey was confused and told his story to his dad. Mr. Williams explained that most countries in the world measure temperature using a scale called Celsius. The United States measures temperature using a scale called Fahrenheit. Mr. Williams went on to say that there is an easy rule to convert temperature in Celsius to Fahrenheit:

$$\text{Fahrenheit} = (9/5) \times \text{Celsius} + 32$$

See if you can help Jeffrey with some questions that came to mind.

1. Costa Rica is located between which two countries? _____

2. Because of Costa Rica's location, what kind of temperature would you expect to find in the country (cold or warm)?_____

3. Why should we care about saving the rain forest in Costa Rica? ____
_____

4. At what temperature Fahrenheit does water freeze? _____

5. At what temperature Fahrenheit does water boil? _____

6. When Jeffrey heard that the temperature was 18 degrees Celsius, what would the temperature be in Fahrenheit? _____

7. At what temperature Celsius would water freeze? _____

8. At what temperature Celsius would water boil? _____

9. Jeffrey made friends with Juanita and explained his temperature confusion to her. Juanita asked Jeffrey for a rule to change temperature from Fahrenheit to Celsius. See if you can find the rule!

_____

Is there a temperature that is the same in both Celsius and Fahrenheit? _____ If so, what is it?_____

Locked in the Mall

Felisha and John were shopping at Sports 4 U. The store was very busy and crowded with customers. The shoes John wanted were not on the floor, so they asked a clerk for help. The clerk took them to the back storage room. Felisha and John were told to go through the boxes to see if they carried the shoes in his size.

Felisha said, "John, I think she just locked the door! We're stuck in this room! What are we going to do?"

"Let's bang on the door until someone hears us." Felisha and John banged on the door with no success. "Well, I guess we're here until someone discovers us," said John worriedly.

Felisha said, "Boy are my parents going to be mad!"

"There's nothing we can do now. Let's try on shoes!" replied John.

Felisha tried on running shoes costing $64.98. She tried on a pair of loafers for $75.45. John tried on three pairs of shoes. The first pair was sneakers for $24.95. The second pair was canvas lo-riders for $19.95, and the last pair was mountain climbers for $99.99.

Felisha said, "Why, John, how do you like these boots?" Felisha had on a pair of real leather boots for $195.00.

"I think my boots are cooler than yours," said John. John had on a pair of snakeskin cowboy boots for $149.99.

John and Felisha tried on shoes until they got tired and fell asleep. They both awoke the next morning when they heard the door latch open. The store manager saw empty shoe boxes and the shoes lying everywhere. "What are you doing here?" shouted the manager.

Felisha and John explained their dilemma. The store manager was so apologetic. He told them to pick out two pairs of shoes each. To be fair, Felisha and John decided to select two pairs of shoes that would cost about the same for each of them.

1. Which pair of shoes did Felisha and John decide to take that would cost about the same amount for both of them? State the shoe name and cost for each. _____

2. The store manager said he would give them the shoes, but Felisha and John would need to pay the sales tax. If the sales tax is 8.5%, how much did Felisha pay? _____ How much did John pay?_____

3. If John and Felisha each paid for the two pairs of shoes, how much would they have paid altogether (including tax)? _____

4. If John and Felisha accepted the most expensive pair of shoes, how much sales tax would they pay? _____

5. What is the difference between Felisha's most expensive pair of shoes and John's most expensive pair of shoes (including tax)? _____

6. If Felisha and John were given every pair of shoes they tried on, how much money did the store owner need to record as a gift (without tax)? _____

The Messy Room

"Cris! Your room is absolutely disgusting! That's it! Tell your friend to go home. We're going to the decorating store. Your room is going to be overhauled," Mom screamed with "the" look.

"O.K., you heard her. You've got to leave," said Cris.

"Wait, Cris, I'll help you," Mike offered.

"Oh, Mike, I'm not sure you want to get into this. Mom has her mind made up about painting my bedroom, and she wants me to do it all. She constantly tells me that I need to take responsibility. She thinks if she makes me paint the room, I'll keep it cleaner," stated Cris.

"I really don't mind. I think it will be fun! Go ask your mom if it's O.K. to help you," said Mike.

Cris's mom agreed to let Mike help, so Cris and Mike began their planning. "Hey, Mike, what color do you think I should paint it?" asked Cris.

"I don't know. What were you thinking about?" inquired Mike.

"Hey, let's create a wild design on one wall and paint the other walls with a cool color, like orange or deep purple!" Cris exclaimed with excitement.

"I bet your mom won't go for that," stated Mike.

Mike was right. Cris's mom said the walls had to be one color and that color had to be a neutral tone. The lecture came. "When you get a house of your own and you pay the rent, you can do anything you want!" fussed Mom.

"Yeah, yeah, yeah," thought Cris.

Cris and Mike were driven to the decorating store to look at paint. Before they left, they measured the walls and the window frames. Two walls were 8¼ feet by 13 feet. The other two walls were 8¼ feet by 10 feet. Cris had two windows that measured 45 inches square. The molding around the window was 3½ inches wide. The window sill measured 5 inches wide.

Cris and Mike chose a pale yellow latex paint for the walls. One gallon of paint covered 450 square feet. Cris's mom insisted that they use two coats of paint to cover the pink that was on the wall now. Cris was also told to paint the window frames with white enamel. Cris and Mike read the label to find that a gallon of white enamel covered 400 square feet.

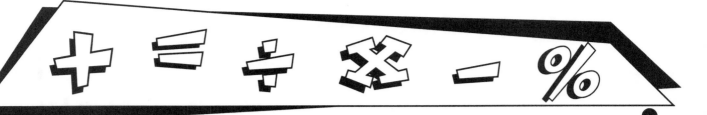

1. Calculate the square footage of the four walls without windows. ____

2. How many gallons of paint will Cris need to buy if she has to paint each wall twice? _____

3. Cris's mom also insisted that she paint the baseboards with white enamel. The baseboard molding is 4" wide. How many square feet of baseboard does Cris need to paint? _____

4. What is the total square footage that needs to be painted with white enamel (include the window frames, sills, and base boards)? _____

5. If 1 gallon of white enamel covers 400 sq. ft., how much will 1 quart cover? _____ Should Cris and Mike buy a gallon or a quart of white enamel? _____ Why? _____
   _____

6. A gallon of pale yellow paint sells for $14.95. A gallon of white enamel sells for $16.49, and a quart of white enamel sells for $8.39. How much will it cost to purchase paint for the room if the walls are painted twice? _____

7. Cris also picked up two rollers at $4.59 each, two paint trays at $1.59 each, two brushes at $4.39 each, and turpentine for $6.50. How much extra did this cost? _____

8. If the sales tax is 4.5%, what is the total cost of painting the room?
   _____

The Combination

It was the first day back from spring break. Trina and Pete were walking to class. "I need to stop by my locker," said Pete. They walked along towards Pete's locker. "Here's my locker. Wait for me. It'll only take a minute."

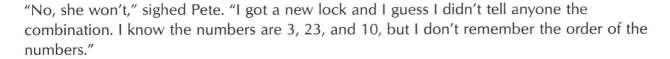

"What's wrong?" asked Trina.

"I can't remember my locker combination!" exclaimed Pete worriedly. "Didn't I give you the combination?"

"No," answered Trina. "Let's go to Mrs. Preston, your homeroom teacher. "She'll have the combination."

"No, she won't," sighed Pete. "I got a new lock and I guess I didn't tell anyone the combination. I know the numbers are 3, 23, and 10, but I don't remember the order of the numbers."

"We can have Mr. Claw, the custodian, cut it off," said Trina.

"Let's go to class and I'll deal with it later," said Pete. After math class Pete talked to his Algebra II teacher and told her the problem.

"Come on, Pete," chided Mrs. Order. "You can figure out the possible number of combinations. Then you can go back and try each one."

"How can I do that?" asked Pete.

"Well, first determine how many arrangements of the three numbers are possible. List each of the possibilities. Since you have only three numbers, it won't be hard," asserted Mrs. Order. "An arrangement of numbers or letters in a particular order is called a *permutation*. The number of possibilities, or the number of permutations of different items, can be determined by using factorials."

"Oh," thought Pete. "I thought it was going to be easy."

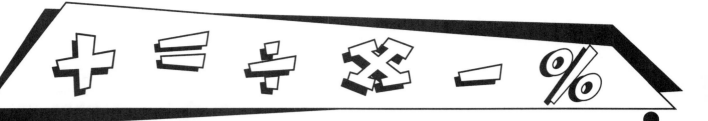

1. "First, list all the possible combinations of 3, 23, and 10," said Mrs. Order. _____

_____

2. "Now, let use math!" Mrs. Order said with a smile. "Suppose you have 4 numbers. To determine how many different ways you can arrange 4 numbers, you can use 4! which means four factorial. Four factorial is the product of all the whole numbers up to and including that number. 4! = 4 * 3 * 2 * 1 = 24. If you had a lock with 4 numbers, there are 24 possible arrangements," said Mrs. Order.

   "Use this concept to determine the exact number of possibilities for your lock combination." _____

_____

3. "What did you find?" asked Mrs. Order. "Now, suppose you had the choice of taking 5 classes in any order. Determine how many different ways you could arrange your schedule," said Mrs. Order. _____

_____

4. "Before I let you go to your locker, tell me why it's important for you to know the mathematics behind the problem," Mrs. Order demanded.

_____

_____

Slammed into the Locker

"Hey, why are you holding your head?" asked Bizz E. Body.

"Someone just slammed me into the locker!" shouted Doreen Clean. "Boy, does my head hurt!"

"Did you see who did it?" asked Bizz.

"Not really, but there were a lot of people in the hall. I bet someone saw who it was," assured Doreen.

"I'll help you find the person," said Bizz.

Gidget Widget walked up to Bizz and Doreen. "What's up?" she asked.

"Did you see someone push me?" asked Doreen.

"No, but someone just ran past me in the hall," said Gidget. "I didn't see who it was, but I know she had brown hair, was wearing a white T-shirt, and had on baggy jeans."

Doreen, Bizz, and Gidget walked through the hall questioning classmates about the incident. Everyone saw something different. One person thought it was a guy with dreadlocks, another person thought it was the custodian, and still another claimed it was the new girl with long blond hair. It seemed as though they would never find the culprit.

Later that day in the lunchroom Jason Cason came up to Doreen. "I heard you got slammed into your locker today," said Jason. "Are you all right?"

"Yeah," whispered Doreen in a low voice. "I wish I knew who did it."

"What would you do if you found out?" questioned Jason.

"I'd slam them right back. I'd rip out their tongue. I'd . . . I'd . . . I guess I'd just report them," sighed Doreen.

"Well, I know who did it. Remember last night when you and Rebecca were on the phone having an argument? I was listening on the extension. She's still mad at you for saying that about her boyfriend. She was bragging about slamming you into your locker today. All the kids in my math class heard it," finished Jason.

"Thank you," said Doreen. "Now all I need to do is report her. She won't be slamming anyone else anytime soon," chuckled Doreen with a satisfied grin.

1. Before Doreen talked to Jason, she had thought about offering a reward for the person who slammed her. Her stepfather, who had a lot of money, just might agree to pay. Doreen imagined that he would pay about 8½ times her age. Since she was 16, how much money would 8½ times her age be? _____

2. Doreen's locker number was an odd number. It was also a prime number and it had 3 digits. The digit in the ones place was 1 less than the digit in the hundreds place. The digit in the tens place was a 7. The digit in the hundreds place was a 2. What was the whole number? _____

3. Doreen's stepfather insisted on taking her to the emergency room for x-rays and a checkup after the incident at school. The doctor said she would need to take 4 pills a day for 3 days, 3 pills a day for 7 days, and 2 pills a day until the medicine ran out. The medicine lasted for 6 more days. How many pills were in the prescription to begin with?

_____

Rebecca admitted that she had slammed Doreen into the locker. She was suspended for disruptive and dangerous behavior during school hours.

4. There were 30 more days left of school for the year. The principal gave her an suspension of 20% of the days left. How long was her suspension? _____

5. Rebecca's parents took her car keys away and fined her ⅕ of her allowance. If at the end of the week she only got $20.00, what was her original allowance? _____

Travis's Dream

Travis's dream was to be in the dirt bike rally held every year in Richmond, Virginia. Travis approached his friend Thomas J. "Hey, T. J., I really think it would be cool to run the dirt bike race in Richmond this year. Do you want to go?"

T. J. replied, "Yeah, that would be great! But I don't know, Travis. My parents are paying to send my sister to summer camp. They don't have any money and I don't either. What about you?"

Travis said, "I'm going! I bet we could save enough money to go. The race is in three months."

"Yeah," replied Travis. "My aunt lives up there. We can stay with her, and my dad said he would drive us. We just need to figure out how much it's going to cost. The registration fee is $75 per person."

"How many days should we stay?" asked T. J.

"Probably at least three days. We should plan to go the day before the race to get our stuff together and then stay one more day after the race to clean everything up," said Travis. "My dirt bike is ready. How about yours?"

"Other than being caked with mud and having two soft tires, I'm ready," replied T. J. "I can be ready in time."

The boys made a list of the things they would need to buy for the race and a list of their expenses at the race. They needed two sets of spare tires for $150, a brake assembly for $35.00, and two spare pedals for $25.95. T. J. needed a new pair of gloves for $15.00.

The boys agreed to take $25 each for expenses at the race. They could purchase something to eat and drink and have money for a T-shirt or a patch for their backpacks.

1. What would be the total cost for the trip to the bike rally in Richmond, Virginia, including the $50 for expenses at the rally? _____

2. The bike rally was 3 months away. Travis decided that he wanted to have at least ¼ of the money by the end of the first month. How much money would this be? _____

3. T. J. found 2 slightly used spare tires for 35% cheaper than the price of $150. What was the price for the 2 slightly used tires? _____

4. T. J. and Travis mowed lawns to make money for the bike rally. They charged $15.00 a week to mow lawns. By the end of the three months they had earned $345 from their lawn venture. How many lawns had they mowed in this period of time? _____

5. At the bike rally T. J., who had a huge appetite, bought 3 giant Buggy burgers, a strawberry shake, and 2 large orders of fries. The total cost of his food was $12.45. Bike rally T-shirts cost $19, and the patch for his backpack would cost $1.75. How much more money does T. J. need to get the T-shirt and patch? _____ If he borrows that amount from Travis, will Travis have enough to get a T-shirt?_____ Should Travis loan T. J. the money? _____

The Big Show

Mrs. Baird called a meeting on Wednesday afternoon to begin planning for the school's annual fashion show for charity. The money was always dedicated to the convalescent home in town. Mrs. Baird asked Colby, Beth, and Katie to attend.

"Girls, here's what I want you to do if you are willing," said Mrs. Baird. "Beth, you will be in charge of the outfits for the show. Colby, you will be responsible for tickets sales, and Katie, I want you to take care of advertising. I've given each of you a big responsibility. I want you to go home to talk with your parents. I will need to know tomorrow if you can do this! What do you think?" Mrs. Baird asked with a smile.

"Oh, sure, Mrs. Baird!" the girls said with excitement.

"This is going to be great!" Beth said.

"Thank you, girls! You're going to have a great time! Just to let you know, the school will contribute $250 for the expenses. If our costs run greater than that, we must pay the remaining expenses from the ticket sales," said Mrs. Baird.

After getting permission from their parents, Beth, Colby, and Katie went to Susie's Cutie Boutique. They spoke to the manager who was more than happy to help the school with outfits. Susie, the manager, said they could have two skirts, three pairs of pants, five shirts, and two jackets.

"Beth, Colby, since we're here in town, let's stop by the printers and see what they will charge for advertising," said Katie.

"O.K., let's go!" replied both girls. They found that a ream of white paper had 500 sheets and cost $6.80. If they decided on colored paper, the cost was $7.59 per ream. The cost of fluorescent paper was even more at $8.38 per ream. The printer told the girls that she usually charged $.07 a copy, but for the school she would only charge $.04 a copy.

The girls also decided to call the local newspaper to see how much it would cost to place an advertisement. The newspaper charged $75/square inch for advertisements, but, again, since this was for the school, the advertising editor told the girl that he would charge them $65/square inch. Also, if the girls wanted the newspaper to design the advertisement, the fee would be $150. Colby suggested, "Hey, let's ask my mom to design our ad for the newspaper. She's terrific and it won't cost us anything."

"That sounds good to me," replied Katie.

"We'd better sit down and look at how much this is going to cost," said Beth.

"We may not be able to advertise in the newspaper. It sure does costs a lot of money!" stated Katie.

"Come over to my house, and we'll talk to my mom and look at what we have so far," said Colby.

1. How many different combinations of outfits can Beth arrange with 2 skirts, 3 pairs of pants, 5 shirts, and 2 jackets? Use a chart to help you determine the possibilities.

2. Katie decided to use color paper for student flyers. If there are 1,200 students in her school, how many reams of paper must she buy? _____ What is the total cost of making 1,200 copies including the cost of the reams of paper? _____ How much money did the printers contribute to the school by allowing the school a discount on copying? _____

3. How much more money did Katie spend by using colored paper instead of white paper? _____ How much money did she save by not using fluorescent paper? _____

4. Colby's mom designed an advertisement that was 2" by 3". How much will it cost to run the advertisement in the paper? _____ How much did the newspaper contribute to the school by allowing a discount on the advertisement? _____

5. Determine the total expenses for the fashion show. _____ Since the school will cover $250 of the expenses, how much of the expenses needs to be covered by the ticket sales? _____

Surfing the Deal

"Hey, Lyonel, I just bought a surfboard for $90!" exclaimed Lisa.

"Let me see," demanded Lyonel. "I can't because I just sold it for $100," said Lisa.

"Why did you do that?" questioned Lyonel.

"I plan to buy it back for $110," explained Lisa.

"I don't understand! Can't you make up your mind?" asked Lyonel.

"Oh, I know what I'm doing!" exclaimed Lisa. "I'm going to sell it again for $120," she remarked.

"Cindy! Hey, come here and listen to what Lisa's done," begged Lyonel. "I think she's been out in the sun too long!" he stated.

"No, I haven't, Lyonel. I plan to make money. I started buying the surfboard for $70, then I sold it for $80, bought it back for $90, and sold it again for $100," explained Lisa. "I just can't figure out how much money I'll be making after I buy it back for $110 and sell it again for $120," puzzled Lisa. "How much money do you think I'll make after selling the surfboard for $120?" questioned Lisa.

"Well, Lisa, it sounds like you are already $30 ahead," stated Cindy.

"I disagree with both of you," said Lyonel. "I think you'll only be $20 ahead if you're lucky enough to sell the surfboard again," figured Lyonel.

Just then Chad walked up and joined the group. "What's up, guys?" asked Chad.

"You won't believe what Lisa is doing!" shouted Lyonel. "She has a plan to make money by selling and buying a surfboard," stated Lyonel. Chad listened to the story.

"She'll make money all right," said Chad. "I did the same thing with a pair of power boosters for my stereo," remarked Chad. "I bought a pair of power boosters for $75, sold them for $85, bought them again for $95, and sold them one more time for $105," stated Chad. "You better be careful Lisa. Not everyone wants a surfboard in the middle of winter," Chad concluded.

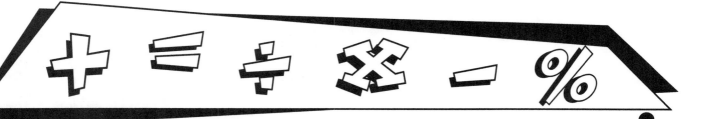

1. When Lisa bought the surfboard for $70 and then sold it for $80, how much money did she make? _____

2. How many times did Lisa buy and sell the surfboard before talking with Lyonel? _____

3. How much money had Lisa made at that point?_____

4. Describe the strategy you used to determine how much money Lisa made. _____

5. At what point did Lisa owe $80? _____

6. If Lisa is successful with her plans, how much money is she going to make? _____

7. Write a mathematical expression using integers that represents all of Lisa's transactions. _____

8. How much money did Chad make when he bought and sold the power boosters? _____

9. Do you think Lisa will be able to sell the surfboard one more time? _____

10. Describe two possible endings for Lisa. _____

_____

_____

Covering the Story

Roger and Maria were a happily married couple. They had known each other since high school. They both worked very hard to provide a good life for their family of three children. The children's names were Paula, Teresa, and William. Roger, Maria, and the children lived in a house that was comfortable for two people but very crowded for the large family of five!

The family saved money and bought a beautiful country house with a large lawn, which the children could use to play soccer. The house had enough room for each child to have his or her own bedroom. Maria particularly liked the large family room. She always wanted a room with Aztec style tile on the floor. Her room in the new house was rectangular in shape. Its dimensions were 24 feet by 12 feet. Maria and Roger went to the tile store to find Maria's dream tile. The store had many designs of Aztec tile that came in squares of various sizes. The design on the tile was so beautiful that Maria could not bear to cut through any of the tiles to make them fit the room.

Maria and Roger took the book containing all the available tile designs and returned home to see what possibilities they could create for their dream family room. Roger gathered all the children to help the family work out all the possibilities that could be considered. He told the family that all the tile designs could be purchased in square sections of various sizes. Maria reminded the family that she refused to cut any of the tiles. It became clear to the family that a little mathematics was required for the family to consider all possible design options.

1. If all the squares are the same size, what is the least number of squares that Roger and Maria can use to cover the floor of the family room? _____

2. How large would the squares be? _____

3. If the squares were in whole number dimensions, what is the largest number of tiles that would be needed to cover the floor? _____
_____

4. How large would the squares be? _____

5. If the family decides to use two different size squares, what could the different squares' dimensions be? _____

6. How many of each size tile would be needed? _____
_____

Sleezy Salesman

Joe Sleeze had been selling magazines for two years. Joe did not go door to door but instead he called poor, unsuspecting clients on the phone with the deal of a lifetime. "I can sell you eight of your favorite magazines for the inexpensive price of only five dollars a week," Joe politely presented his proposition to the client. "Now where in the world can you find a better deal than eight newsstand magazines for a measly five bucks?" Joe questioned the prospective buyer. "Check any counter at any hotel or airport or check at Waldart or Q-mart and see if you can come up with a better price for any eight magazines of your choice."

"That's exactly what we will do, Wilma!" Mr. Slow enthusiastically explained to his wife of 22 years.

In short order, Mrs. Slow was quick to investigate newsstand prices and to make some startling discoveries! "If I purchased select publications for one year from the local newsstand on the corner of Speedy Boulevard and Fast Track Lane, I would pay $15.00 a year for *Family Square*, $12.00 for *Blue Book* and $10.00 a year for *Woman's Way*. Gosh, I just always figured I was getting a deal when I stopped there and picked up something with a snappy cover," a surprised Mrs. Slow reported back to Mr. Slow.

"You know, I investigated and have discovered that if I were to stop by that same newsstand on the way home from work to select some of my favorite publications, I would end up paying $25.00 a year for *Consumer Import*, $15.00 for *Car and Back-Seat Driver,* and $30.00 a year for *Meadow and River*," a perplexed Mr. Slow said as he scratched his balding head.

Junior quickly joined in, "I can buy *Ranger Sick* for $10.00 a year and *Lowlights* for $15.00 a year from that same newsstand. I heard you talking and I already checked."

"Maybe this Mr. Sleeze does have a real deal for the Slows," Father pondered.

Mrs. Slow was quick to respond, "Clarence, don't we need to investigate further?"

"Yes, dear, I do think we need to know more," Mr. Slow reassured Wilma. "Tomorrow I fully intend to check the cover prizes of our favorite magazines with Publisher's Cleaning House."

Publisher's Cleaning House was quick to report to Wilma Slow that their prices were the same as the newsstand cost. However, if Mrs. Slow ordered more than five magazines from the company, the Slow family would receive a ten percent discount on the price of each magazine subscription. In the meantime, Mr. Slow discovered that he could receive a ten percent discount on his three magazines if he ordered them from his place of work. Junior investigated and discovered that he could order his two favorite magazines at school with a twenty percent discount.

"Our family has four options," Mr. Slow explained to his family at dinner. "First option is our family buys all their magazines from the local newsstand. Second option, we could purchase all the family's magazines from the Publisher's Cleaning House. Third option, Mother can purchase her three magazines from Publisher's Cleaning House, I can buy my three choices from work, and Junior can buy his two from school. Finally, our fourth option is that the Slow family buy all their magazines from Joe Sleeze."

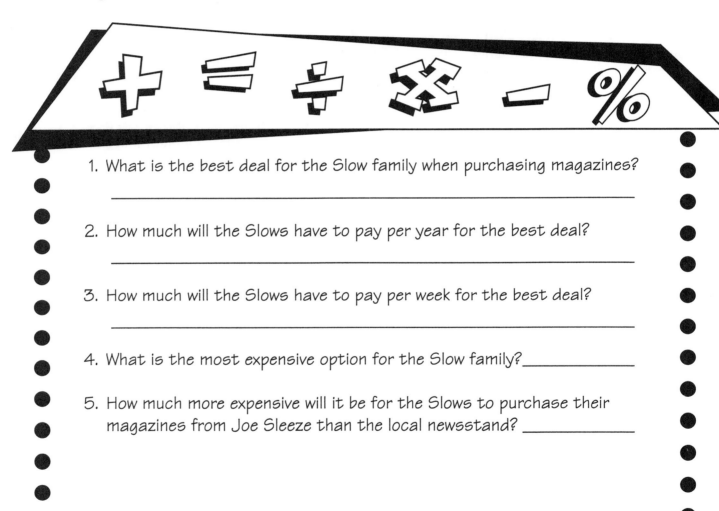

1. What is the best deal for the Slow family when purchasing magazines?

   _____

2. How much will the Slows have to pay per year for the best deal?

   _____

3. How much will the Slows have to pay per week for the best deal?

   _____

4. What is the most expensive option for the Slow family?_____

5. How much more expensive will it be for the Slows to purchase their magazines from Joe Sleeze than the local newsstand? _____

Munchin' Luncheon

Kenny, Cassandra, and Kendall were made to go to breakfast with their dad on Sunday morning. "I'm going to teach you something today," stated Dad. "Oh, Dad, not again!" exclaimed Cassandra. "Dad, don't you ever get tired of teaching us—we always complain!" stated Kendall. Kenny just slouched down in the seat looking disgusted.

Dad drove them to the Beach Cafe. Cassandra whispered to Kenny, "How are we going to get him to let us eat in peace?"

"Come on, Kenny, think of something!" said Kendall.

Kenny remained silent for a few minutes but then whispered, "Give it up and let's play his game. You know he won't change his mind."

They arrived at the Beach Cafe and were seated outside on the deck. The bright, warm sun and the cool, gentle breeze helped improve everyone's attitude. "OK, kids, here's the plan," said Dad. "There are four of us for breakfast. I have $40 to spend. The three of you will be responsible for determining what we can order including sales tax and tip."

Kenny spoke to his dad in a funny yet sarcastic tone, "Dad, does that mean we can decide what you can eat or not eat?" Kenny's dad just gave him a look.

"No, Kenny, I will have the Sunday steak and eggs brunch with coffee," replied Dad.

Beach Cafe Menu

Sunday Brunch

Steak & Eggs	$6.95
Eggs Benedict	$6.95
Western Omelette	$6.95
Seafood Omelette	$6.95
Meat Lover's Omelette	$6.95
Crab Benedict	$7.95
Waffles	$5.95

Two Eggs—any style	$5.95
Side Orders	$1.50
(Bacon, Sausage, Ham)	
Beverages	
Coffee or Tea	$1.00
Soft drinks	$ .75
Juice	$1.00

1. If the total bill came to $22.45, determine the sales tax (9%) and the total bill. _____

2. How much tip should they leave the waiter (20% of the bill for the tip; round the answer to the nearest dollar)? _____

3. What is the total cost of the bill including tax and tip (round answer from problem 2)? _____

4. How much change will their dad receive from his two $20 bills? _____

5. If Dad ordered the steak & egg brunch with coffee, determine how much his breakfast will cost with tax included. _____

6. How much money is left for Kendall, Cassandra, and Kenny to order their breakfasts? _____

7. If they divide this amount evenly, about how much can each spend? _____

8. If Kendall ordered waffles and juice, Cassandra ordered scrambled eggs and a soda, and Kenny ordered the meat lover's brunch and juice, compute the bill including Dad's breakfast. Compute the sales tax at 9% and add in the tip (20%) rounded to the nearest dollar. _____

9. Will they have enough money to pay for the meal with tax and tip included? _____

10. How much change will they receive? _____

11. What other possibilities could the children order and not exceed $40?

_____

Once on the Lips, Twice on the Hips

Steffy turned 16 on January 9, and the very next day she had a job at Doumar's Ice Cream Parlor. They had so many delicious flavors including Strawberry Sundae, Peachy Keen, and To-Die-For Chocolate. Sometimes a customer would ask to try a particular flavor, and Steffy would give them a sample in a little cup. The only problem was that every time she gave someone a sample, she took some herself. That was in addition to all the ice cream she brought home to try in the evenings.

After about two months on the job, Steffy noticed that her baggy jeans were no longer baggy. "They must have shrunk in the wash," she explained to Pam, her best friend. Then her long black belt that hung down to her knees, now fit with just two inches to spare. "My dog Skipper probably chewed off the end," Steffy said to Pam.

By May Steffy was really having a problem finding clothes in her closet that hadn't shrunk. "It must be the new detergent Mom's using," she thought. In the meantime, Doumar's started making ten new flavors, and Steffy couldn't decide whether Heavenly Blueberry Pie or Out-of-This-World Coffee ice cream was her favorite. So to solve the problem she kept tasting spoonfuls of both.

The mystery of the shrinking clothes came to a head one day in June when Steffy and Pam were putting on their bathing suits to get ready for a pool party. "Look at this old two-piece bathing suit," complained Steffy. "I feel like I'm wearing a girdle."

"You are," noted Pam. "There's more of you hanging out of that bathing suit than is in it. Face it, Steffy. That job at Doumar's has packed on about 25 pounds, and it's all sitting on your hips."

1. Steffy started the job on January 9. She didn't know it, but she was packing on about 4 lbs. a month. How much did she gain from January 9 until June 9? _____

2. The accounting records at Doumar's revealed that 27 gallons of ice cream were sold the first week Steffy worked there, 32 the second week, 30 the third week, and 35 the fourth week. If this pattern continues, how much ice cream will be sold the next week? _____

3. One day Steffy made Pam a triple scoop of blueberry, vanilla, and peach ice cream. The only problem was that Pam couldn't decide in what order to put the 3 flavors. How many different ways could she stack the scoops? Try to use factorials to figure out the answer. _____

4. Steffy showed Pam a photograph of herself before she packed on the extra pounds. The photograph was 6¼ inches by 3⅕ inches. How big was the photograph in square inches? _____

5. One day Steffy got an unusual shipment of ice cream. The containers were ⁷⁄₁₀ of a gallon, ³⁄₅ of a gallon, ⅓ of a gallon, and ⅞ of a gallon. Order the containers from smallest to largest. _____

Saving the Earth

Tanisha was so surprised when her teacher began the day's lesson by explaining how much goes into creating the air that we breath. Tanisha thought to herself how she takes the air for granted and just figured that it always was here and always will be! She could not wait to go home and tell her mother all that she had learned. The teacher assigned a project for each student to work on at home. The school day ended and Tanisha hurried on the school bus to make the journey home to her mother.

"Mama, Mama," Tanisha yelled. Her mother came running to see what had her daughter so excited. Tanisha told her mother the story that her teacher had shared with the students. The air we breath depends on the supply of oxygen in the atmosphere. This balance is partially controlled by the amount of rainforests that exist in the tropical zone of our planet. The teacher also explained that some countries are destroying the rainforests that are located within their borders. The land is used for cattle to graze and for farmers to grow much needed crops to feed the people of the country. Most countries have no plans to replenish the land that has been taken from the rainforests. Other countries, like Costa Rica, are doing their best to restore the rainforests that are located within their borders.

Tanisha's teacher gave the class an assignment. The teacher began with some important information. She told the class that a country had lost 55,000 acres of rainforests to development over the past 11 years. This year, the people of the country voted to continue to restore lost rainforest land at the same yearly rate that it had been lost over the past 11 years. The government also began a policy of creating national parks of rainforests at the rate of 10,000 acres a year. The teacher asked the students to answer a few very important questions about the future of rainforests in this country.

1. Over the past 11 years, what was the average yearly acreage of rainforests lost to development?_____

2. What is the new yearly ratio of land taken from rainforests to new land dedicated to rainforests? _____

3. Does this ratio mean that overall for each year we *gain* or *lose* land to development? _____ By how much acreage? _____

4. How many years will it take to reclaim all the rainforest lost over the past 11 years? _____

5. Over the next 20 years, how much land will be reclaimed for the rainforests? _____

6. What are some other reasons why we should be concerned with the loss of land to rainforests?_____

    _____

    _____

Tina's Mom

Tina was very happy to see the rain begin on a Saturday in June. Normally, she would be sad to see the rain because it would stop Tina from going outside to play with her friends. The difference today was the fact that her mother had promised her that on the first Saturday that it rained, Tina and her mother would make Tina's favorite dessert from scratch. This special dessert is called Brazilian Chocolate.

Tina and her mom went to the store and purchased all the ingredients that they would need to make the recipe. The recipe serves 4 people, and the ingredients include the following:

Melt in a double boiler over hot water:
1 oz. chocolate
$\frac{1}{4}$ cup sugar
$\frac{1}{8}$ teaspoon salt

Add and stir in:
1 cup boiling water

Continue to heat 3 to 5 minutes. Add:
$\frac{1}{2}$ cup hot milk
$\frac{1}{2}$ cup hot cream
$1\frac{1}{2}$ cups freshly made hot strong coffee

Beat mixture well and add:
1 teaspoon vanilla

1. If the recipe serves 4 people, what would you do to each ingredient if you wanted to serve 8 people? _____

2. How much of each ingredient would you need? _____

_____

_____

3. If the recipe serves 4 people, what would you do to each ingredient if you wanted to serve 2 people?_____

4. How much of each ingredient would you need? _____

_____

_____

5. If the recipe serves 4 people, what would you do to each ingredient if you wanted to serve 20 people? _____

6. How much of each ingredient would you need? _____

_____

_____

Happy Mother's Day

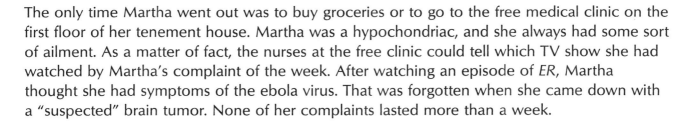

Martha Strayer lived in the heart of Chicago on the twenty-seventh floor of a tenement house. She had thousands of neighbors in the 30-story building, but not one friend. It was a lonely life, but gray haired and stoop-shouldered Martha had her cats. Everywhere you looked around her apartment, you saw cats. Tabby cats on the counter, Siamese cats on the chairs and couches, and stray cats of all sizes and colors scattered here and there.

The only time Martha went out was to buy groceries or to go to the free medical clinic on the first floor of her tenement house. Martha was a hypochondriac, and she always had some sort of ailment. As a matter of fact, the nurses at the free clinic could tell which TV show she had watched by Martha's complaint of the week. After watching an episode of *ER*, Martha thought she had symptoms of the ebola virus. That was forgotten when she came down with a "suspected" brain tumor. None of her complaints lasted more than a week.

Martha had two sons and a daughter, but they lived in California and rarely visited. "Here Tabby, Tabby," said Martha in her sweet frail voice. "Mommy loves you, sweetheart."

It was Mother's Day and Martha was feeling lonelier than ever. Her two sons and daughter hadn't even called or sent cards or flowers. They usually did, so Martha was beginning to feel a sickness coming on. Just then the doorbell rang.

"Hi, Mom," said Sarah with Martha's sons, Steve and Jerry, standing right behind her.

"We decided to come out together and surprise you on Mother's Day," announced Steve. "We have a whole day planned just for you." Martha forgot all about feeling sick.

Martha was ecstatic and for one glorious day she had no complaints, as she was pampered with dinner at a fancy restaurant and a trip to the botanical gardens. When she visited the free clinic the next week, all she could talk about were her kids and the Mother's Day celebration.

1. In the apartment, Martha had 27 cats in all. Someone complained and the landlord came and told Martha that she could keep only $\frac{1}{3}$ of her cats, or he would fine her $2.00 a day for each cat over the $\frac{1}{3}$ that she was allowed. If it took Martha 2 weeks to find good homes for her extra cats, how much was the fine? _____

2. Martha was mixing some dry cat food with milk one day. The directions said to mix 1 part dry cat food with 3 parts milk. If Martha used 8 cups of dry cat food, how much milk would she have to use? _____

3. One day when Martha was especially bored, she decided to count pieces of cat food that came in a 10-lb. bag. The pieces were really small, and she counted 1,476,453 before lunch. After lunch she continued counting and reached another really big number 68,578. Finally, before she went to bed, she finished counting the very last piece. She counted 20,567. How much does she have altogether? _____

4. Martha's children Sarah, Steve, and Jerry each paid a different amount for their flights. Sarah used a Frequent Flyer Coupon so she had 45% off the regular price of a flight. Steve flew first class so his ticket cost $100 more than a regular price ticket. Jerry was the only one to pay the regular price for his ticket, which was $645. How much did Sarah and Steve pay for their flights? _____

5. A palindrome is a number like 1001 or 23532, that reads the same backwards or forwards. What if Martha had saved 12,021 pennies for a trip out to California to visit her children? How many more pennies must she save before she comes up with another palindrome? _____

_____

Answer Key

Sara's Pet   **Page 2**
1. 14 dog years; chart: 1—7, 2—14, 3—21, etc.
2. $25.00 per month
3. 672 square feet, 654 square feet
4. 2 years old, 14 dog years
5. 512 bunnies the third year

The Pesky Neighbor   **Page 4**
1. 4 pkgs. of hot dogs and 5 pkgs. of buns
2. $12.51, $10.51
3. $5.00, 20 quarters, 50 dimes, 100 nickels
4. about 90 centimeters
5. 4, $1.50

Every Girl Needs an Allowance   **Page 6**
1. 9 years old and 6 years old, $7.00
2. $10.75, yes
3. 12—$20.00
   13—$21.60
   14—$23.33
   15—$25.20
   16—$27.22
4. $13.88
5. 2 out of 6 chances, 1 out of 6, 2 out of 5, 1 out of 5

Bullfrogs and Winged Bugs   **Page 8**
Yes, temperatures were warm enough to open the pool.
1. mean—90°, median—91°, mode—there is none range—10°
2. 205
3. 22
4. 17; yes, if both dates are within the same month
5. $35.38, yes $.50 per gallon
6. 7 out of 11, 4 out of 11

Leo's Room   **Page 10**
1. $20.00, $15.00
2. $12.00 per hour
3. 51 minutes
4. about 66 kilograms
5. 50 times, 1,000 minutes, 2
6. $2.50

The Bull's-eye   **Page 12**
1. 300
2. There are many combinations.
3. 10, 10, 10, 10; 30, 20, 20, 10; or 20, 20, 20, 20
4. 220

5. $11.25, no
6. $25.00

School Clothes   **Page 14**
1. 6, 12 with and without a belt
2. $15.00 each
3. $9.00
4. 2
5. Amber at $21.60 per pair
6. 2 hours 50 minutes, 5:05

Report Card Time   **Page 16**
1. 74
2. 6, 80%
3. to lose 2 weeks of allowance, $51.92 more, 6 weeks
4. 78
5. 86

Michael's Pentium Pro   **Page 18**
1. $3,651.70
2. $152.15 per month
3. $703.00
4. 48 years old
5. $166.00
6. 555-3142

Lucky Clyde Clevermore   **Page 20**
1. 3 square inches
2. $5.00—5 cans of soda and 25 quarters
   $10.00—10 cans of soda and 50 quarters
   $20.00—20 cans of soda and 100 quarters
3. seventh set equals 49 clovers, 1, 4, 9, 16, 25, 36, 49, 64, 81, 100
4. octagon—8 sides, nonagon—9 sides, pentagon—5 sides, decagon—10 sides
5. 32

The Surprising Soccer Game   **Page 22**
1. 2x - 3; 69, 71, 73, 75, 77, 79, 81, 83, 85, 87; 9 players
2. 35
3. 80% won, 20% lost
4. final quarter 32
   (first quarter 128, second quarter 96, third quarter 64)
5. all players play 2 quarters, 10 people play 3 quarters

Eloise's Helpful Hints   **Page 24**
1. 6 combinations
2. 12 sandwiches
3. mean 30.2, median 30, mode 32, range 4
4. about 14.6% of her day
5. 10%
6. 2:51

Go Wildcats!   **Page 26**
1. 1 cut 2 pieces, 2 cuts 4 pieces, 3 cuts 6 pieces, 4 cuts 8 pieces, 5 cuts 10 pieces, 6 cuts 12 pieces, 7 cuts 14 pieces, 8 cuts 16 pieces, 9 cuts 18 pieces, 10 cuts 20 pieces.
2. 93.43 miles per hour
3. .142857142857
4. 407 batting average
5. .090909
6. 20, 22, 24; John's number is 22

Luciano's Pizzeria   **Page 28**
1. 50.27 inches
2. 7 inches
3. 2 large pepperoni pizzas at $17.48, 3 large sausage and pepper pizzas at $28.47, 2 cheese pizzas at $15.98, and 1 large special at $15.98 for a total of $77.91
4. 12% of $77.91 equals $9.35 so they pay $68.56 before taxes. Tax $5.48 for a total bill of $74.04.
5. 3 Fifth Street, 4 Napoli Avenue, 7 San Paolo Street, 21 Italiano Street

A Bundle of Nerves   **Page 30**
1. 6 white cars
2. $\frac{1}{5}$, 30 bald men
3. MATHEMATICS IS FUN!
4. 18 minutes late
5. small suitcase 15 lbs., medium suitcase 25 lbs., and large suitcase 40 lbs.
6. 25 which is 5 squared

Vinnie's New Job   **Page 32**
1. 18.84
2. 10 (If cheese is included, the answer is 15.)
3. $.12/minute, $207.36, take-home pay
4. 212.6 eggs, the restaurant should buy at least 89 dozens of eggs
5. 324, 5 hours and 24 minutes, he should start at 7:36

Surprise Birthday Party   **Page 34**
1. 72 sq. inches minus 12.57 inches equals 59.43 sq. inches for writing
2. $19.75 price of the cake

3. writing cost $2.84
4. 5,400 sq. inches
5. 20 balloons for $4.50
6. 4, 7 tables

Growing Gladiolus   **Page 36**
1. 1$\frac{7}{8}$ hours
2. $90.00 for bulk
3. $.07 per oz.
4. purple, orange, blue, red, yellow
5. $1.20 end of the day price
6. 2 months

The Magic Sneakers   **Page 38**
1. $15.99
2. 12:15 or 3:00
3. 3 sq. cm
4. $4,549.50
5. $3,370.00

Alien Invasion   **Page 40**
1. $1\frac{1}{2}$ oz.
2. $1.60
3. $\frac{1}{6}$
4. 6 days
5. $12.35 for all the candy
6. 5,764,801 people

Vacations Are Supposed to Be Fun   **Page 42**
1. 2:00 P.M.
2. $320
3. galoshes $8 (umbrella $4, raincoat $36)
4. 39 degrees
5. 4$\frac{5}{6}$ feet

The Teddy Bear Collection   **Page 44**
1. if there is no leap year: 3,650 days, 87,600 hours, 5,256,000 minutes
2. 120 different ways
3. about 3 kilograms
4. about 726 kilograms and a little over 3 meters
5. The real Kodiak brown bear is huge and dangerous.

Curing a Couch Potato   **Page 46**
1. 144 oz. or 4260 ml
2. cheaper to buy 3—2 liter bottles of Coke, $.72
3. 4 quarts or 1 gallon
4. the dress weighed 907.18 grams
5. about 10 miles

Crazy About Geometry   **Page 48**
1. 5,000 lbs. or 2,270 kilograms
2. 6.28 cm

3. 10.5 minutes
4. $24.00
5. 36 degrees
6. 3,261 years

The Weirdest Emergency   Page 50
1. 4, 5, 1 across and 2, 5, 3 down; there are more possible answers
2. 1 lb. of ground beef
   6–32oz. cans of kidney beans
   ½ c. of chopped onions
   2 cans of stewed tomatoes
   2–6 oz. cans of tomato paste
   1⅓ tsp. of garlic powder
   ¼ tsp. of salt
   7 tsp. of chili powder
3. 4 cans
4. 12 out of 52
5. $15.00

Jacob Asternaut's Sleep Problems   Page 52
1. ⅙ for elephants and giraffes
   ⅓ for humans
2. 16,975 minutes
3. x = 7
4. human 5:30 A.M., cat 3:30 P.M.
5. $540.00

Easy Money   Page 54
1. 16 years old
2. $27.50
3. $2.75
4. 3 and 5
5. 4 more hours

Cloud Watching   Page 56
1. 6:21
2. 12 bulls, ⅞
3. $564, 96
4. $14,630
5. 5,280 feet

Cookie on a Cattle Drive   Page 58
1. 10:45
2. 4 gallons, Jasper's hat
3. $14.16
4. $3.045 or $3.05
5. $1.55

Harry's Hair Dilemmas   Page 60
1. 1,000 hairs
2. 5,000 hairs
3. 80%
4. 16 months
5. $680.00

6. $510.00
7. 4,000 hairs

Spreading the News   Page 62
1. 2,187 people
2. 2,379 people
3. 3,379 people

Ida Mae and the College Fund   Page 64
1. $1.50
2. $511.50
3. $65,535.50
4. Ida Mae can attend the college with a tuition of $8,593.00, and Ida Mae can attend the college with a tuition of $14,991.00.
5. all three schools

Sneak Previews   Page 66
1. 2,000 seats
2. 93 people
3. 127 people
4. 655 people
5. two theaters
7. $11,000.00

The Daytuna 500 Race   Page 68
1. 1.5 minutes
2. 80 times around
3. 2 hours, Yes
4. 40 times
5. 1 hour
6. 160 gallons

One Hundred Hungry Ants   Page 70
1. Yes
2. 64 ants
3. 40 ants
4. No
5. 130 ants
6. 18.4 ounces
7. More than three days (3.68)

Rocky's Roads   Page 72
1. 15 porters
2. three
3. 10 porters
4. 6 porters
5. 20 porters

Something's Fishy   Page 74
1. 60%
2. 100%
3. 40%
4. 31.5 pounds
5. 70 pounds
6. 13.5 pounds

7. $57.50
8. 50 cents

The Boring Trip   Page 76
1. $450.00
2. white
3. 48.6%
4. red and silver
   4.3%
5. west
6. 40
7. 30
8. Pete

Freddie's Fertilizer   Page 78
1. 15,000 square feet
2. 15,000-square-foot bag
3. $160.00 per year
4. $2400.00 per year
5. $150 per year
6. Billie Bob
7. Barefeet Lawn Service

Cookies a Plenty   Page 80
1. yes
2. 760 points
3. Marsha
4. 65 boxes
5. Tina
6. 220 points
7. devil's food
8. macaroons

Nicole's Adventure   Page 82
1. a. -1
   b. +2
   c. -2
   d. +3
2. Sports Center

The Tampa Experiment   Page 84
1. The group should consider the profit from each item, the amount of traffic passing the location, and the amount of available parking.
2. The amount of profit from each fruit juice is $.25 - $.05 or $.20.
   The amount of profit from each candy bar is $.25 - $.15 or $.10.
   The amount of profit from each cookie is $.25 - $.20 or $.05.
3. The profit from 50 fruit juice is 50 x .20 or $10.00.
   The profit from 50 candy bars is 50 x .10 or $5.00.
   The profit from 50 cookies is 50 x .05 or $2.50.

4. The best plan is the fruit juice sale suggested by Kelly. The fruit juice earns the most profit from each item sold. There is good traffic flow and there is sufficient parking spaces for cars.

A Calculating Dilemma   Page 86
1. Nicaragua and Panama
2. warm
3. Scientists find sources of medicine from the plants in the rain forest. Many animals are facing extinction. Many meteorologists feel that weather patterns are affected by the rain forests.
4. 32 degrees
5. 212 degrees
6. 64.4 degrees
7. 0 degrees
8. 100 degrees
9. Celsius = ⅝ x (Fahrenheit - 32)
10. yes, -40 degrees

Locked in the Mall   Page 88
1. Felisha took a pair of boots ($195) and the sneakers ($64.98). John took the cowboy boots ($149.99) and the mountain climbers ($99.99).
2. Felisha paid $22.10 in tax. John paid $21.25 in tax.
3. The total altogether is $553.31.
4. $29.33, Felisha would pay $16.58 for the boots. John would pay $12.75 for the cowboy boots.
5. The difference between the most expensive pairs of shoes is $48.84.
6. The total amount of the shoes is $630.31.

The Messy Room   Page 90
1. 379.5 square feet
2. 2 gallons
3. 15⅛ square feet
4. approximately 25 square feet
5. 100 square feet; a quart. One quart will complete the task.
6. $38.29
7. $27.64
8. $68.90

The Combination   Page 92
1. 3, 23, 10; 3, 10, 23; 23, 10, 3; 23, 3, 10; 10, 23, 3; 10, 3, 23
2. 3! = 3 * 2 * 1 = 6
3. 5! = 5 * 4 * 3 * 2 * 1 = 120
4. It is important to know the mathematics because you can find the answer faster and be more accurate.

Slammed into the Locker   **Page 94**
1. $136.00
2. 271
3. 45 pills
4. 6 days
5. $25.00

Travis's Dream   **Page 96**
1. $425.95
2. $106.49
3. $97.50
4. 23
5. $8.20 more. No, because then he wouldn't have enough money to buy his own lunch.

The Big Show   **Page 98**
1. 60 combinations
2. 3 reams of paper; $70.77; $36.00
3. $2.37; $2.37
4. $390; $60
5. $460.77; $210.77

Surfing the Deal   **Page 100**
1. $10
2. She bought it twice and sold it twice.
3. $20
4. made a chart
5. after she bought it back for $90
6. $30
7. -70 + 80 - 90 + 100 - 110 + 120
8. $20
9. Answers will vary.
10. Lisa will own a surfboard paying $90, or she will be $30 ahead without the surfboard.

Covering the Story   **Page 102**
1. 2 tiles
2. 12 feet by 12 feet
3. 288 tiles
4. 1 foot by 1 foot
5. Answers will vary.
   Sample answer: Tile 1: 6 feet by 6 feet; Tile 2: 12 feet by 12 feet
6. 4 tiles of 6 by 6 and 1 tile of 12 by 12

Sleezy Salesman   **Page 104**
1. Option #2
2. $118.80 per year
3. $2.28 per week
4. Joe Sleeze
5. $128.00 per year

Munchin' Luncheon   **Page 106**
1. $2.02, $24.47
2. $5.00
3. $29.47
4. $10.53
5. $8.67
6. $31.33
7. $10.44
8. $29.55, $2.66 tax, $6.00 tip, total bill $38.21
9. yes
10. $1.79
11. Answers will vary.

Once on the Lips, Twice on the Hips   **Page 108**
1. 20 lbs.
2. 33 gallons of ice cream
3. 6 different combinations
4. 20 sq. inches
5. $\frac{1}{3}$, $\frac{3}{5}$, $\frac{7}{10}$, $\frac{7}{8}$

Saving the Earth   **Page 110**
1. 5,000 acres
2. 500:1,000 or 1:2
3. gain, 5,000 acres
4. 11 years
5. 100,000 acres
6. Medicine from the trees, effects on world temperatures, effects on weather patterns, loss of animal and plant species.

Tina's Mom   **Page 112**
1. Multiply each amount by 2 or add each amount to itself.
2. Melt in a double boiler over hot water:
   2 oz. chocolate
   ½ cup sugar
   ¼ teaspoon salt
   Add and stir in:
   2 cups boiling water
   Continue to heat 3 to 5 minutes. Add:
   1 cup hot milk
   1 cup hot cream
   3 cups freshly made hot strong coffee
   Beat mixture well and add:
   2 teaspoons vanilla
3. Multiply by ½ or divide by 2.
4. Melt in a double boiler over hot water:
   ½ oz. chocolate
   ⅛ cup sugar
   ¹⁄₁₆ teaspoon salt
   Add and stir in:
   ½ cup boiling water

Continue to heat 3 to 5 minutes. Add:
   ¼ cup hot milk
   ¼ cup hot cream
   ¾ cup freshly made hot strong coffee
Beat mixture well and add:
   ½ teaspoon vanilla
5. Multiply by 5.
6. Melt in a double boiler over hot water:
   5 oz. chocolate
   1¼ cups sugar
   ⅝ teaspoon salt
Add and stir in:
   5 cups boiling water
Continue to heat 3 to 5 minutes. Add:
   2½ cups hot milk
   2½ cups hot cream
   7½ cups freshly made hot strong coffee
Beat mixture well and add:
   5 teaspoons vanilla

Happy Mother's Day   **Page 114**
1. $504
2. 24 cups of milk
3. 1,565,598 pieces of cat food
4. Jerry $645, Steve $745, Sarah $354.75
5. 100 more pennies before she would have 12121